Benjamin C. Ray

The old Battle Flags

Veteran Soldiers' Souvenir

Benjamin C. Ray

The old Battle Flags
Veteran Soldiers' Souvenir

ISBN/EAN: 9783337120443

Printed in Europe, USA, Canada, Australia, Japan

Cover: Foto ©ninafisch / pixelio.de

More available books at **www.hansebooks.com**

PROGRAMME.

LINE OF MARCH, COLLATION, ETC.

The Veteran Soldiers will meet on BUSHNELL PARK at 10.30 A. M., hold their regimental meetings, and organize for the march, which will be in the following order:

1st Company Governor's Horse Guards,
MAJOR BOARDMAN.

1st Company Governor's Foot Guards,
MAJOR GEORGE B. FISHER.

Putnam Phalanx,
MAJOR BROWN.

1st Regiment Conn. National Guards,
COL. L. A. BARBOUR.

Veteran Soldiers in the numerical order of their Regiments.

THE LINE OF MARCH

will be from the Park up High street to Main, to the Arsenal, and countermarching, each regiment will receive the old flag—borne, as far as possible, by the men who carried them in the field—and move down Main street to Park street, to Washington street, to the Capitol, amid the ringing of bells and firing of cannon.

Upon the arrival at the Capitol the flags will be presented by General HAWLEY, and received by Governor ANDREWS, each flag receiving an artillery salute.

After the ceremonies a bountiful collation will be given to the soldiers by the citizens of Hartford, in large tents pitched on the Park.

A Triumphal Arch will be erected in front of the new City Hall (old State House), and the city will be gaily decorated.

AUTHOR'S OVERTURE.

The transfer of the Old Connecticut Battle Flags from the State Arsenal to the new Capitol building, where they will remain a perpetual memorial of the State's loyalty and patriotism, seems to the author an appropriate occasion for reproducing in a brief and authentic manner the history of the various regiments which so gallantly upheld the honor of Connecticut during the war for the preservation of the Union. No State was more loyally represented in the field than Connecticut, and her flag never faltered where the foes of the Union were to be met. On the historic battle-grounds of the war Connecticut won imperishable glory. And now, after fourteen years of peace, the heroes of the struggle assemble to look once more upon the torn and tattered colors which they bore through a hundred fields of conflict, rallying with all the old time enthusiasm around them. Every soldier will recognize the fitness of the author's effort in compiling this little volume, which is offered as a tribute to the day now to be celebrated. He has confined himself to such facts as could be obtained from official records and other sources at command, avoiding all romance. Doubtless there may be errors and omissions, but he trusts to the generosity of his fellow soldiers to overlook whatever faults the work may contain.

> "Flag of the free heart's hope and home!
> By angel hands to valor given;
> Thy stars have lit the welkin dome,
> And all thy hues were born in heaven.
> For ever float that standard sheet!
> Where breathes the foe but falls before us,
> With freedom's soil beneath our feet,
> And freedom's banner streaming o'er us."

Opening Chorus: Battle Cry of Freedom!

Yes, we'll rally round the Flag, boys,
We'll rally once again,
   Shouting the battle-cry of Freedom!
We will rally from the hill-side,
We will rally from the plain.
   Shouting the battle-cry of Freedom!

CHORUS.—The Union for ever, hurrah! boys, hurrah!
   Down with the traitors! up with the stars!
While we rally round the Flag, boys,
Rally once again,
   Shouting the battle-cry of freedom.

We are springing to the call
Of our brothers gone before,
   Shouting the battle-cry of Freedom!
And we'll fill the vacant ranks
With a million freemen more,
   Shouting the battle-cry of Freedom!

CHORUS.—The Union for ever, hurrah! boys, hurrah! etc.

We will welcome to our number
The loyal, true, and brave,
   Shouting the battle-cry of Freedom!
And although he may be poor,
He shall never be a slave,
   Shouting the battle-cry of Freedom!

CHORUS.—The Union for ever, hurrah! boys, hurrah! etc.

Yes, for Liberty and Union,
We are springing to the fight,
   Shouting the battle-cry of Freedom!
And the victory shall be ours,
For we're rising in our might.
   Shouting the battle-cry of Freedom!

CHORUS.—The Union for ever, hurrah! boys, hurrah! etc.

FIRST REGIMENT (3 Months).

This Regiment sprang to arms at the first sound of war, and left New Haven for Washington, May 9, 1861, under command of Col. Daniel Tyler, who on the 10th of May was promoted to be Brig.-General, and at the battle of Bull Run was in command of a Division.

Col. George S. Burnham, his successor, had been connected for a number of years with the State volunteer organizations, and he was in command at the battle of Bull Run, where he was conspicuous for his bravery, and where he and his command acquitted themselves with honor to the cause in which they were engaged.

July 21st the regiment advanced on the Warrenton road toward Bull Run, where the enemy was entrenched. After marching and counter-marching, at times under severe fire, until 4 o'clock P. M., it was ordered to retreat, which it did in splendid order, saving large quantities of stores though hotly pursued by the victorious foe ; its loss was eight wounded and nine missing.

Resting at Centreville, the regiment returned to its old camp at Falls Church, reaching there July 23d, when their tents were struck, where they remained during the day exposed to a drenching rain, occasioning much suffering on account of the very fatiguing duties of the previous day, and need of rest.

George H. Bugbey, Co. A, of this Regiment, was the first Connecticut soldier wounded in the war for the preservation of the Union, his left shoulder being badly lacerated at Vienna, Va., June 16, 1861. Mr. Bugbey is the present Armorer at the State Arsenal, by appointment of Quartermaster-General Wessells.

The Regiment was mustered out of service at New Haven, July 31, 1861, having fulfilled its mission with credit to itself and to the State.

SECOND REGIMENT (3 Months).

This Regiment left New Haven for Washington, May 10, 1861, 780 men, under command of Col. Alfred H. Terry, who was for a number of years an able and efficient officer in the State Military organizations.

At the commencement of the war he was Colonel of the 2d regiment State Militia, and was very popular with his command.

The regiment was engaged in the disastrous battle of Bull Run, and acquitted itself with the coolness, courage, and bravery of old veterans. A great many of its members afterwards saw service during the darker days of the war.

The regiment was highly disciplined, and reflected great credit on the State. It was mustered out of service August 7, 1861, at New Haven.

BUY YOUR FAMILY STORES
—AT—
The BOSTON BRANCH

TEA & GROCERY HOUSE,
273 MAIN STREET.

THE ONLY GENUINE BOSTON GROCERY HOUSE in Hartford.

CHOICE TEAS A SPECIALTY!

FLOUR RETAILING AT WHOLESALE PRICES:

You can buy *FIRST CLASS GOODS* at LOW PRICES, and you only have to pay for your own goods, as we sell strictly *for Cash*, making no bad debts to cover by over-charging paying customers.

Call for Catalogue of Prices. We Warrant every article we sell.

CANNED GOODS Lower than the Lowest.

TRY OUR 50 CENT TEA.
COFFEE! COFFEE! COFFEE!

Every pound of COFFEE sold by us is Ground in our Store as it is sold.

GIVE US A CALL, and you will see at a glance that

YOU CAN GET MORE GOODS for YOUR MONEY THAN EVER BEFORE, at the

Boston Branch Tea and Grocery House,
273 MAIN ST., HARTFORD.
J. P. HAYNES & CO.

THIRD REGIMENT (3 Months).

The Third Regiment left Hartford for Washington May 25, 1861, under command of Col. John Arnold. Col. Arnold tendered his resignation May 29, 1861, on account of ill health.

He was succeeded by Col. John L. Chatfield, afterward Col. of the Sixth Regiment, who died Aug. 9, 1863, from wounds received at Fort Wagner.

The Regiment was in the battle of Bull Run, and was highly complimented for its steadiness and gallantry under the enemy's terrible fire.

It was mustered out at Hartford, August 12, 1861.

FIRST SQUADRON CAVALRY.

This organization was recruited by Capt. Mallory of Hartford, to compose a part of a volunteer regiment of Cavalry to be raised in different States, with the understanding that it was to be distinctly a Connecticut organization; but it was afterwards assigned to New York and known as the 2d New York Cavalry (Harris Light Cavalry), whose fortunes it followed during the war. No official report of its operations was received, and no reliable summary of events or operations can be given, beyond that as a regiment it was noted for its bold dash and daring in the various actions in which it was engaged.

It was mustered out of the service June 23, 1865.

R. H. DOUTHWAITE & SON,

DEALERS IN

Foreign & Domestic Fruit,

CONFECTIONERY, etc.,

210 Main Street,   Hartford, Conn.

FIRST CONN. CAVALRY.

The First Cavalry was originally a batallion of four companies, one from each Congressional District, and was organized in the Fall of 1861. It left West Meriden for Wheeling, Va., Feb. 20, 1862, 346 men, where they remained in camp of instruction until March 27.

The battalion under Major Lyon took an active part in the battle of McDowell, May 3, and also in the operations which terminated in the battle of Franklin, May 11 and 12, 1862.

It also served in the army of Gen. Fremont, then in command of the Mountain Department, in his forced march across the mountains into the Shenandoah Valley to the relief of Gen. Banks, participating in the battles of Harrisonburg, June 6, Cross Keys, June 8, and Port Republic, June 9.

It subsequently took part in the arduous operations of the army of Virginia under Gen. Polk, participating in the various battles along the Rapidan and the Rappahannock, and at Bull Run and Chantilly.

After nearly a year of constant activity the batallion was assigned to duty as Provost Guard in the city of Baltimore, and was increased to a full regiment of 12 companies.

In February, 1863, the regiment was attached to the Army of the Potomac, and took an active part in all its movements, until August 8, 1864, when it was transferred to the army of the Shenandoah.

History alone can do full justice to the brave men who composed this magnificent regiment. Suffice it to say that while under Gen. Sheridan it maintained a reputation for fidelity and bravery second to no other Cavalry regiment in the war.

The regiment continued in service under Cols. Ives and Whittaker until Aug. 2, 1865, performing gallant service, winning a well-merited reputation, and doing honor to the State that sent it into the field.

It was mustered out at Washington, D. C., Aug. 2, 1865, and left for New Haven for final discharge. The members of the regiment were permitted to take their horses with them to the State, a favor which was not granted to any other cavalry regiment.

SOME OF ITS PRINCIPAL ENGAGEMENTS.

McDowell, Va., May 8, 1862; Franklin, Va., May 11 and 12, 1862; Strasburg. Va., June 1, 1862; Harrisonburg, Va., June 6, 1862; Cross Keys, Va., June 8, 1862; Port Republic, Va., June 9, 1862; Bolivia Heights, Va., July 14, 1862; Waterford, Va., Aug. 7, 1863; Craig's Church, Va., May 5, 1864; Spottsylvania C. H., Va., May 8, 1864; Meadow Bridge, Va., May 12, 1864; Hanover C. H., Va., May 31, 1864; Ashland, Va., June 1, 1864; near Old C. H. Tavern, Va., June 10, 1864; in the field, Va., June 15 to June 28, 1864; Ream's Station, Va., June 29, 1864; Winchester, Va., Aug. 16, 1864; near Kernysville, Va., Aug. 25, 1864; Front Royal, Va., Sept. 21, 1864; Cedar Run C. H., Va., Oct. 17, 1864; Cedar Creek, Va., Oct. 19, 1864; near Woodstock, Va., Nov. 24, 1864; Waynesboro, Va., March 2, 1864; Ashland, Va., March 14, 1865; Five Forks, Va., April 1, 1865; Sweat House Creek, Va., April 3, 1865; Harper's Farm, Va., April 6, 1865.

ITS CASUALTIES.

Killed in action, 24; died of wounds, 8; died of disease, 125; discharged prior to muster out, 436; missing at muster out, 59. Total, 652.

FIRST LIGHT BATTERY.

The First Connecticut Light Battery left the State for Port Royal, S. C., January 13, 1862, numbering 156 men.

It remained in the department of the South until April 18, 1864, when it left Folly Island for Fort Monroe, arriving there April 22d. It disembarked at Gloucester Point on the 23d, and reported to Gen. Terry, commanding forces at that point.

On the 4th of May it again embarked on transports, and on the 6th of May landed at Bermuda Hundred, and took up a line of march for Richmond and Petersburg road.

On the 10th of May it took an active part in the battle of Chester Station, and notwithstanding the efforts of the enemy, who charged the Battery three times during the engagement, the casualties were but two men wounded.

On the 13th of May it was transferred to the Eighteenth Army Corps, and placed in position on the Richmond and Petersburg turnpike. It was, however, ordered back to the Eighteenth Corps on the 14th, in time to participate in the battle of Proctor's Creek. The Battery was engaged in active service from this date until October 29th, when it was ordered to City Point for the purpose of exchanging guns.

On the 4th of December the Light Artillery Brigade of the Tenth Army Corps and the Battery took up its position in the rear of Fort Bunham, near James River, doing excellent service in the army of Virginia, until its muster out, June 11, 1865.

In December, 1863, forty-six of its original members re-enlisted as veterans.

ITS PRINCIPAL ENGAGEMENTS.

James Island, S. C., June 14, 1862; *Secessionville, S. C.*, June 16, 1862; *James Island, S. C.*, July 10, 1863; *John's Island, S. C.*, February 10, 1864; *Proctor's Creek, Va.*, May 14, 1864; *Four Mile Creek, Va.*, August 14, 1864; *Siege of Petersburg, Va.*, August 27 to September 27, 1864; *Darbytown Road, Va.*, October 13 and October 27, 1864.

CASUALTIES.

Died of Wounds,	1
Died of Disease,	21
Discharged prior to muster out,	98
Total,	120

CHARLES E. REICHE'S
OYSTER HOUSE & LUNCH ROOMS,
627 MAIN ST., HARTFORD, CT.

THE FINEST OYSTERS IN EVERY STYLE AT ALL HOURS.

Choice Lager, Wines, Liquors & Cigars.

OYSTERS

For the Season of 1879-80

AT THE

OLD FAIR HAVEN OYSTER STAND,

No. 30 State Street,

Under United States Hotel,   HARTFORD, CONN.

Stores, Hotels, Restaurants, Festivals, and Families supplied on the best of terms with

Oysters Opened from the Shell

by the gallon, quart, or pint, fresh every day from Fair Haven, Stony Creek, Norwalk, &c.
Also, the celebrated Maryland Oysters, in their season.

LONG AND ROUND CLAMS

in their season, delivered free to any part of the city.

Orders solicited from old and new patrons, and it will be our aim to give satisfaction to all who will favor us. Connected with District Telephone, and orders received through that source will be promptly attended to.

Respectfully yours,

THOS. A. HONISS.

THE DAY OF JUBILEE!

Soldiers of the Revolution, Soldiers of the War of 1812,
SOLDIERS OF THE WAR FOR THE UNION!
Soldiers of the Home Guard, Soldiers of the next War,

WHILE VISITING HARTFORD ON

BATTLE FLAG DAY,

OR AT ANY OTHER TIME,

WILL FIND THE

U. S. Hotel Billiard Room

A very nice quiet place to enjoy a

GAME OF BILLIARDS OR POOL.

Choice Wines, Cigars, etc.

42 STATE STREET, U. S. HOTEL.

FRANK L. AVERY, Manager.

FIRST REG'T HEAVY ARTILLERY.

The First Regiment Heavy Artillery was organized as the Fourth Regiment Infantry, in the Spring of 1861, and left for the seat of war June 10th, 1861. It served as an Infantry regiment until Jan. 2d, 1862, when it was changed to Heavy Artillery, of 12 companies of 150 men each.

The Regiment was stationed in the fortifications about Washington, but at the commencement of the Peninsular campaign, the regiment, under command of Col. Rob't O. Tyler, accompanied the army with a siege train of seventy-one pieces of artillery. It signally distinguished itself in the seige of Yorktown, and in the engagements at Hanover Court House, Gaines' Mills, Malvern Hill, and Chickahominy, and its gallantry was recognized by an order directing these engagements to be emblazoned on its colors. Its high character had been so well sustained, that it was ranked, by competent military judges, as the best volunteer regiment of heavy artillery in the field, and worthy of imitation.

The reasons mentioned for its superiority, were the material in physique and intelligence, and its thorough drill and excellent discipline, acquired under Col. Tyler. This regiment furnished to other organizations the following officers, who served with distinction in the field: Lieut. Col. Perkins, Major Clark, and Capt. Gibbons of the 14th; Major Washburn and Capt. Mix of the 16th ; Lieut. Col. Kellogg and Capt. Ellis of the 19th regiment (2d Artillery).

On the 19th of Nov. 1862, Col. Tyler was promoted to be Brig.-General, and Capt. H. L. Abbott of the U. S. Topographical Engineers was appointed to the command.

On the withdrawal of the army from the Peninsula, the regiment was ordered to the forts at Washington, with the exception of two companies, which remained with the army of the Rappahannock, and took part in the bombardment of Fredericksburg.

On the 10th of May, 1864, the regiment was ordered to report to Gen. Butler, then near Bermuda Hundred, Va., where they arrived May 13th about 1700 strong, but 349 men were discharged in ten days thereafter, their term of service having expired. The regiment was, however, soon recruited to the maximum. The Third Conn. Independent Battery was temporarily attached to the regiment on the 15th day of November.

In January, 1865, a portion of the regiment accompanied the siege train commanded by Col. Abbott, whose destination was Fort Fisher. On the 15th of January, Fort Fisher having been carried by assault, the train returned to the old lines.

With a regiment so widely scattered as was this, unusually responsible duties devolved upon subordinate officers, all of whom were highly spoken of by Col. Abbott, who at the same time praised the enlisted men for the laudable manner in which they seconded the efforts of their officers, and for their cool bravery while under the enemy's fire. Major-Gen. W. T. Smith wrote to Col. Abbott, " I saw much of the service of the First Connecticut Artillery, and was surprised and delighted with the skill and gallantry of the officers and men. During the time I commanded the 18th Army Corps before Petersburg, I called heavily upon you for siege guns and mortars, and never during

war have I witnessed such glorious artillery practice as I saw with your regiment; the practicability of holding my position there after the 1st of June was due to the great skill and valor of your noble regiment."

The regiment served with the Army of the Potomac and the Army of the James, until the evacuation of Petersburg and Richmond by the rebel forces in 1865, returned to Washington, and on the 25th of Sept., 1865, was mustered out, after having done battle for the Union four years and four months.

The Regiment has been in the following ENGAGEMENTS:

Siege of Yorktown, Va., April 30 to May 4, 1864; *Hanover Court House, Va.*, May 27, 1862; *Gaines' Mills, Va.*, May 31 to June 20, 1862; *Chickahominy, Va.*, June 25, 1862; *Golden Hill, Va.*, June 27, '62; *Malvern Hill, Va.*, July 1, '62; *Siege of Fredericksburg, Va.*, Dec. 11 to Dec. 15, 1862 (Batteries B and M); *Before Fredericksburg, Va.*, April 28 to May 6, '63 (Battery M); *Before Fredericksburg, Va.*, June 5 to June 13, 1863 (Battery M); *Kelley's Ford, Va.*, Nov. 7, 1863 (Battery M); *Orange Court House, Va.*, Nov. 30, 1864 (Battery B); *Siege of Petersburg and Richmond, Va.*, May 1864, to April, 1865 (11 months active operations); *Fort Fisher, N. C.*, Jan. 14 and 15, 1865.

Its Aggregate Number of Casualties.

KILLED IN ACTION, - - 26	DIED OF DISEASE, - - 161
DIED OF WOUNDS, - - - 23	DISCHARGED (before muster-out), 1071
TOTAL, - - - - - 1281	

SOLDIERS OF THE REPUBLIC!

DEFENDERS OF THE OLD FLAG!

Who gather to do Honor to the OLD BATTLE FLAGS,

And all others visiting Hartford, will find good

BOOTS AND SHOES

At BOTTOM PRICES at the

New England Boot and Shoe House,

354 MAIN STREET,

(Cor. Kingsley,)   HARTFORD, CONN.

SECOND REG'T HEAVY ARTILLERY.

This regiment was recruited in Litchfield County, as the 19th Regiment of Infantry, and was commanded by Col. L. W. Wessells, the present Quartermaster-General of the State. The regiment left for Washington, on the 15th of Sept. 1862 ; it was assigned to the Army of the Potomac, and stationed at Alexandria, Va.

November 22d, 1863, the regiment was changed to an Artillery organization, and was subsequently designated by Gov. Buckingham as the Second Heavy Artillery. During 1863, it was engaged in garrison duty in the "Defenses of Washington, South of the Potomac," in Forts North, Ellsworth, Lyon, Weld, Farnsworth, Williams, and Willard, and was in the same Brigade with the First Connecticut Artillery, forming the 2d Brigade of DeRussey's Division.

May 21st, 1864, the regiment was assigned to the 2d Brigade, 1st Division, 6th Army Corps, and was continually on the march from that time to the 1st of June, when they were engaged in the Battle of Cold Harbor, Va., suffering a heavy loss, in killed and wounded, of brave soldiers ; among the slain were Colonel Elisha S. Kellogg and Capt. Luman Wadhams ; the total loss of the regiment in that sanguinary battle was 285 killed, wounded, and missing.

The regiment remained with the 6th Corps until the close of the war, taking an active and prominent part in the engagements about Petersburg, and was mustered out of service on the 18th of August, 1865, at Washington, D. C., having struggled bravely for the perpetuity of the Republic, 2 years and 11 months. The muster-in rolls of the 19th regiment Conn. Infantry bore the names of 891 men, but upon the change to Artillery, a large number of recruits were added to its ranks ; and the whole number of men who served in this organization was 2,719 officers and men.

The official reports of the regiment being to a certain extent incomplete, it is hardly possible to place upon record as full a report of its engagements as the long and arduous services of the brave officers and men who composed it so truly merit ; but the gallant deeds of the Second Connecticut Artillery has added a brilliant page to the history of the good old Commonwealth.

Its principal ENGAGEMENTS were

Cold Harbor, Va., June 1, 1864,	Total Loss,	285.
Hatcher's Run, Va., February 6, 1865,	" "	7.
Near Petersburg, Va., March 25, 1875,	" "	20.
Near Petersburg, Va., April 2, 1865,	" "	8.
Sailors Creek, Va., April 6, 1865,	" "	7.

Its CASUALTIES were

KILLED IN ACTION,	143.
DIED OF WOUNDS,	80.
DIED OF DISEASE,	186.
DISCHARGED PRIOR TO MUSTER-OUT,	908.
Total,	1318.

DUFFY'S
ORIGINAL

PINT MUG HOUSE,

18 MARKET ST., HARTFORD.

SMITHS'
New York PALE ALE
AND PORTER,

From McPherson & Donald Smiths' celebrated Brewery, 240 West 18th St., New York.

The Coldest Drink known to mankind.

A PINT MUG ONLY 5 CENTS.

QUART MUG 8 CENTS.

Also, a Selected Stock of WINES, LIQUORS & CIGARS.

Respectfully,

STEPHEN DUFFY, Prop'r,

18 Market St., Hartford.   *Veteran, Co. F, 5th Reg. Conn. Vols.*

FIFTH REGIMENT INFANTRY.

This Regiment left Hartford for the theatre of war July 29, 1861. March 17, 1862. Col. Ferry was promoted to be Brigadier-General, and Lieut.-Col. George D. Chapman to be Colonel.

Under Col. Chapman the regiment saw much active service, and performed more exhaustive marches than almost any other regiment from the State, having marched more than 1500 miles, at one time marching for 29 consecutive days, and in one day the unusual distance of 45 miles. On leaving the State it reported to Gen. Banks, then at Harper's Ferry.

March 1st, 1862, it crossed the Potomac at Williamsport, Md., drove the enemy from Winchester, which they occupied, but on May 24th, after a hard fought battle, was obliged to recross the Potomac, with the entire army. The reports of Brigade and Division Commanders mentioned the gallant Fifth as deserving of the highest praise for the conduct displayed in that battle.

It again went into action at Cedar Mountain, August 9th, with about 400 men, and fought most gallantly, every officer but three, that entered the fight, being either killed, wounded, or taken prisoner.

It was also with McClellan when he moved into Maryland. The day before the battle of South Mountain it was detached in Frederick City for Provost duty, remaining nearly 3 months. Again on the 1st, 2d, and 3d of May, the Fifth was engaged in the battle of Chancellorsville, and acquitted itself with marked distinction. July 1st, 2d, and 3d it participated in the memorable battle of Gettysburg, but from the peculiar disposition of its forces, its loss was very slight—three wounded and five missing.

In December, 1863, the regiment was transferred to the "Department of the Cumberland," and shortly afterwards accompanied Gen. Sherman in his grand march through Georgia and the Carolinas.

May 15th, 1864, it participated in the battle of Resaca, Ga., losing in killed and wounded 51 officers and men. Again on the 25th of the same month it was in the battle of Dallas, Ga. It also took part in the battles of Marietta, Peach Tree Creek, and Atlanta, Ga., Chesterfield C. H., S. C., and Silver Run, N. C., which was its last engagement with the enemy.

Company F of this Regiment had a somewhat remarkable recruit in the form of a dog, who was enrolled at Manchester, March 19, 1862, under the cognomen of "Black Dog Jack." "Jack" followed the fortunes of the Company through all its battles, marches, etc., a faithful companion at all times, and showed a decided antipathy to the boys in grey on many occasions. "Jack" was sent home in care of Sergeant Simonds, and for aught we know is living to-day, enjoying his many "trials and triumphs."

July 19th, 1865, the regiment was mustered out of service, leaving behind them a record of valor that Connecticut may well be proud of. ALL HONOR TO THE PLUCKY FIFTH!

ITS TWENTY ENGAGEMENTS:

Winchester, Va., May 25, 1862; *Cedar Mountain, Va.*, Aug. 9, 1862; *Chantilly, Va.*, Sept. 1, 1862; *Chancellorsville, Va.*, May 1, 2, and 3, 1863; *Gettysburg, Pa.*, July 1, 2, and 3, 1863; *Resaca, Ga.*, May 15, 1864; *Cassville, Ga.*, May 19, 1864; *Dallas, Ga.*, May 25, 1864; *Lost Mountain, Ga.*, June 15, 1864; *Kenesaw Mountain, Ga.*, June 22, 1864; *Culp's Farm, Ga.*, June 22, 1864; *Marietta, Ga.*, June 22, 1864; *Peach Tree Creek, Ga.*, July 20, 1864; *Siege of Atlanta, Ga.*, August to September, 1864; *Monteith Station, Ga.*, Dec. 15, 1864; *Siege of Savannah, Ga.*, December, 1864; *Chesterfield Court House, S. C.*, Feb. 4, 1865; *Silver Run, N. C.*, March 2, 1865; *Averysboro, N. C.*, March 16, 1865; *Bentonville, N. C.*, March 19, 1865.

The wounds of this Regiment were invariably in the body front.

ITS AGGREGATE NUMBER OF CASUALTIES.

KILLED IN ACTION, - - 73	DIED OF DISEASE, - - 81
DIED OF WOUNDS, - - 29	DISCHARGED (before muster-out), 600
Total, - - - - 783	

MARCHING THROUGH GEORGIA.

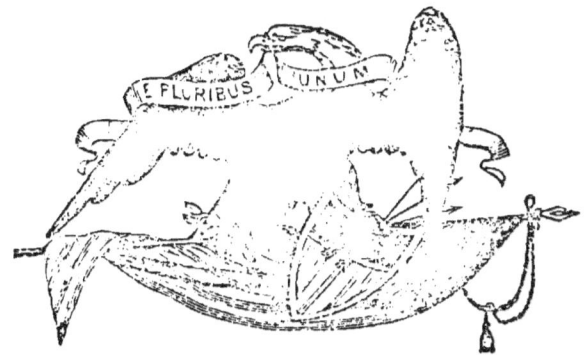

Bring the good old bugle, boys, we'll sing another song,
Sing it with a spirit that will start the world along,
Sing it as we used to sing it fifty thousand strong,
While we were marchin' through Georgia.

CHORUS.—Hurrah! Hurrah! we bring the jubilee!
Hurrah! Hurrah! the flag that makes you free!
So we sang the chorus from Atlanta to the sea,
While we were marching through Georgia.

How the darkies shouted when they heard the joyful sound!
How the turkeys gobbled which our Commissary found!
How the sweet potatoes even started from the ground!
While we were marching through Georgia.

CHORUS.—Hurrah! Hurrah! etc.

Yes, and there were Union men who wept with joyful tears,
When they saw the honor'd Flag they had not seen for years;
Hardly could they be restrained from breaking forth in cheers,
While we were marching through Georgia.

CHORUS.—Hurrah! Hurrah! etc.

Sherman's dashing Yankee boys will never reach the coast!
So the saucy rebels said; and 'twas a handsome boast—
Had they not forgot, alas! to reckon with the host,
While we were marching through Georgia.

CHORUS.—Hurrah! Hurrah! etc.

So we made a thoroughfare for Freedom and her train,
Sixty miles in latitude—three hundred to the main;
Treason fled before us—for resistance was in vain,
While we were marching through Georgia.

CHORUS.—Hurrah! Hurrah! etc.

SIXTH REGIMENT INFANTRY.

The Sixth regiment Connecticut Volunteers, Col. John L. Chatfield, left New Haven Sept. 17, 1861, 1008 men. It was assigned to the Department of the South, and connected with the expedition which resulted in the battle of James Island, June 14, 1862 ; it was in the battle of Pocotaligo, Oct. 22, 1862, in which it lost 33 men, killed and wounded ; Col. Chatfield and Lieut. Col. Speidel were severely wounded ; it also participated in the attack upon the fortifications around Charleston, and the commanding General reports it as having shown great efficiency and bravery in the assault upon the Batteries on Morris Island, July 10th and 18th, 1863.

In the second assault on Fort Wagner, Col. Chatfield, while leading his brave men to the charge, was severely wounded and carried from the field; he returned home to Waterbury, and died August 9, 1863. Thus was lost to the service one of the bravest of Connecticut's brave men.

October 27, Col. Duryee assumed command, and on May 29, 1864, resigned on account of ill health, and was succeeded by Col. Rockwell.

April 27, 1864, the regiment left Hilton Head, S. C., for Fortress Monroe, arriving May 1st, and proceeded to Gloucester Point, and was assigned to the 10th Army Corps. It at once advanced to Bermuda Hundred, and moved into the interior, where it was engaged in the destruction of the enemy's railroads, and harrassing their forces.

On the 13th, the regiment was assigned to Col. Alford's Brigade, Gen. Turner's Division, 10th Army Corps, and ordered to the skirmish line, where it remained to the 16th continually under fire from the enemy's pickets; on the 20th it was engaged in the charge upon and capture of the enemy's line of rifle pits. From this time until January, 1865, it continued its operations in southeast Virginia, and took part in several sharp engagements before Petersburg and Richmond.

In January it was ordered to Wilmington, N. C., and on the 15th was engaged in the battle and capture of Fort Fisher.

In December, 1863, 205 of its original members re-enlisted as veterans August 21, 1865, the Sixth was mustered out of service.

The dash, daring, and heroism displayed by the Sixth, under any and all circumstances, makes a record to which they may point with pride, and which will ever redound with honor to every member of that gallant organization.

ITS PRINCIPAL ENGAGEMENTS.

Pocotaligo, S. C., Oct. 22. 1862; *Morris Island, S. C.,* July 10, 1863: *Fort Wagner, S. C.,* July 18, 1863; *Chester Station, Va.,* May 10, 1864; *Near Bermuda Hundred, Va.,* May 10 to June 18, 1864; *Deep Run, Va.,* Aug. 14 to Aug. 18, 1864 ; *Fort Fisher, N. C.,* Jan. 15, 1865.

ITS CASUALTIES.

KILLED IN ACTION,	- - 43	DIED OF DISEASE,	- - - 119
DIED OF WOUNDS,	- - 46	DISCHARGED prior to muster-out,	663
	Total,	- - 871.	

Capitol City Restaurant

AND
LAGER BEER HALL,

No. 374 ASYLUM STREET,

Headquarters for the Celebrated

PILSNER BEER

From the Lion Brewery, New York.

☞ This celebrated Beer is made of imported German Barley and the finest Hops. Chemists testify to its Purity and Healthfulness, and Connoisseurs prefer it to any other Lager.

Billiard and Pool Tables.

The Finest Place of Resort in Hartford.   Everything first-class

GOERZ BROTHERS, Propr's.

374 Asylum St., (Batterson's Block,) Near Depot.

SEVENTH REGIMENT INFANTRY.

This regiment left for Washington, under command of Col. Alfred H. Terry, with Joseph R. Hawley as Lieut.-Col., with 1013 men. It was in the expedition to Port Royal, and was the first to land and plant its colors on the soil of South Carolina. Upon the receipt of the news, the Governor caused congratulatory orders to be issued announcing the fact, and to be read to each Conn. Regiment in the field. The regiment was in the battle of Fort Pulaski, April 10 and 11, 1862. On the 19th of May following, Col. Terry was promoted to be Brigadier-General, and Lieut.-Col. Hawley was promoted to the colonelcy of the regiment.

June 14, 1862, the regiment was engaged in the battle of James Island, and suffered severely, being one of the first to enter the action, and one of the last to leave the field. In an official report dated June 14, 1862, Colonel Hawley spoke in the highest terms of the gallant and fearless conduct of both officers and men.

October 22d the regiment was again engaged in the battle of Pocotaligo; subsequently the regiment was divided, and on April 1st five companies were at Hilton Head, under Colonel Hawley, the remainder with Lieut.-Col. Gardiner, at Fernandina, Florida.

July 10 and 11, Companies A, B, I, and K were present and took active part in the battles of Morris Island and Fort Wagner; the loss in the two days' fight was 111 men. Capt. Gray in his official report, dated July 13, 1863, speaks in the highest terms of the bravery of the officers and men of the detachment. The loss of officers was terribly severe. Capt. Gray mentions the fact that of eleven officers in his mess but four were left. The Seventh Connecticut Regiment was declared by Gen. Strong "to have covered itself with glory."

From this time until May 4, 1864, it was engaged in active service, performing the arduous duties attendant upon "life in the field." In May it was transferred to Bermuda Hundred, Va., and on the 10th of that month was in the battle of Chester Station, and from that time until the 17th was engaged with the enemy near Bermuda Hundred (incurring an aggregate loss of 196 officers and men). On the 2d and 17th of June it was again engaged near Bermuda Hundred (losing 124 men).

Aug. 14th and 15th it bore a prominent part in the battle of Deep Bottom, Va., and on the 18th that of Deep Run, Va.

Sept. 17, 1864, Col. Hawley was promoted to be Brig.-General, and the command devolved upon Lieut.-Col. Rodman. Sept. 29th it was engaged in the battle of Chapin's Farm, Va.; on the 1st of October in the battle near Richmond; on the 7th, New Market Roads; on the 13th, Darbytown Road, and on the 27th in the battle of Charles City Road, Va. After this brilliant record of battles in Virginia, the regiment was called upon to do battle in another department, and in January, 1865, it was engaged in the capture of Fort Fisher, N. C.

It was mustered out of service July 20, 1865, having fully sustained its reputation as a "fighting regiment," and returned to their homes, receiving the grateful plaudits of their fellow citizens for a soldier's duty nobly done.

ITS NINETEEN PRINCIPAL ENGAGEMENTS.

Fort Pulaski, Ga., April 10 and 11, 1862; James Island, S. C., June 14, 1862; Pocotaligo, S. C., Oct. 22, 1862; Morris Island, S. C., July 10, 1863; Fort Wagner, S. C., July 11, 1863; Olusta, Fla., Feb. 24, 1864; Chester Station, Va., May 10, 1864; Near Bermuda Hundred, Va., May 10 to May 17, 1864; again, June 2, 1864; again, June 17, 1864; Deep Bottom, Va., Aug. 14, 1864; Deep Run, Va., Aug. 18, 1864; Chapin's Farm, Va., Sept. 29, 1864; Near Richmond, Va., Oct. 1, 1864; New Market Road, Va., Oct. 7, 1864; Darbytown Road, Va., Oct. 13, 1864; Charles City Road, Va., Oct. 27, 1864; Fort Fisher, N. C., Jan. 15, 1865; Fort Fisher, N. C., Jan. 19, 1865.

ITS CASUALTIES.

Killed in Action, 90; Died of Wounds, 44; Died of Disease, 179; Discharged prior to muster-out, 587; Total, 940.

EIGHTH REGIMENT INFANTRY.

This regiment was recruited at Camp Buckingham, Hartford, and left for Annapolis Oct. 17, 1861, Col. Edward Harland commanding.
It was engaged in the battle of Newberne, N. C., March 14, 1862, and again at the seige of Fort Macon, N. C., April, 1862.

September 17, 1862, it was engaged in the sanguinary battle of Antietam, where it suffered severely, losing in killed one commissioned officer (the brave and intrepid Lieut. Marvin Wait), 33 men; wounded, 10 commissioned officers, 129 enlisted men.

December 11th and 13th the regiment was again engaged at Fredericksburg, Va., but sustained a small loss. In February, 1863, it was transferred to Southeast Virginia, where it remained until its muster out. Col. Harland having been promoted to be Brig.-General, the command devolved upon Lieut.-Col. Ward, who was promoted to Colonel April 2, 1863.

The regiment participated in the battle of Fort Hugar, Va., April 11 and 19, 1863. On the 11th of January it returned to Connecticut on furlough, 310 of its original members having re-enlisted as veterans. It returned to its old camp near Portsmouth, Va., March 1st, 1864. March 13th it was ordered to Deep Creek, Va. April 13th it shared in the reconnoissance toward Suffolk. May 7th it participated in the battle of Walthall Junction, Va., sustaining another severe loss. It was complimented by its Brigade commander, General Burnham, for heroism that day; and as it returned from the field was cheered by the whole Brigade. Official reports said "it earned its laurels dearly."

From May 9th to May 12th it was engaged in reconnoisance, and from the 12th to the 16th of May, 1864, it was engaged in battle at Fort Darling, and on the night of the 16th it retired within the fortifications, completely exhausted and worn out with its arduous labors. For eight days out of ten it had been in the front, sustaining an aggregate loss of 140, or nearly one-third of its whole fighting strength.

June 1st to June 10th it was engaged with the enemy at Cold Harbor, sustaining a loss of 40 in killed and wounded. Again, from the 13th to the 17th, it was engaged in battle near Petersburg.

June 21st the regiment marched back in front of Petersburg, entered the trenches, and shared in the monotonous siege work until August 27th.

August 27th to Sept. 28th the regiment encamped on the south side of James river, behind the fortifications. At dawn on the 29th the army advanced toward "Battery Harrison." The Eighth furnished two companies of skirmishers, the balance of the regiment heading the storming column. The regiment sustained a loss of 73. This was the last general engagement of the regiment, which was mustered out on the 12th of December, 1865.

That the Eighth Connecticut fully sustained the reputation of Connecticut soldiers for daring, bravery, and fidelity, will never be questioned.

ITS PRINCIPAL ENGAGEMENTS.

Newberne, N. C., March 14, 1862; Fort Macon, N. C., April. 1862; Antietam, Md., Sept. 17, 1862; Fredericksburg, Va., Dec. 11 and 13, 1862; Fort Hugar, Va., April 11 and 19, 1864; Walthall Junction, Va., May 7, 1864; Fort Darling, Va., May 12 to 16 (inclusive), 1864; Cold Harbor, Va., June 1 to 10 (inclusive), 1864; near Petersburg, Va., June 15 to 17 (inclusive), 1864, and June 17 to Sept. 28, 1864; Fort Harrison, Va., Sept. 29 to Oct. 24, 1864.

ITS CASUALTIES.

Killed in action, - - - 72	Died of disease, - - - 132
Died of wounds, - - - 40	Discharged prior to muster out. 610
Total, - - - 854	

NINTH REGIMENT INFANTRY.

This regiment was organized as an Irish regiment and commanded by Col. Thomas W. Cahill, an able, popular, and efficient officer in the State Volunteer Militia. It left the State for Lowell, Mass., Nov. 4th, and on the 21st embarked from Boston for Ship Island, numbering 845 men.

During the battle of Baton Rouge, La., Gen. Williams, commanding the forces, was killed, and the command devolved upon Col. Cahill, leaving Lieut.-Col. Fitzgibbons in command of the regiment. In his official report of this battle, the commanding officer speaks of the conduct of the 9th Connecticut as deserving great credit for its coolness and bravery. Owing to the inaccuracy of the enemy's aim and especially their over-shooting, the casualties were much lighter than might have been expected in so severe an engagement. On the 24th of June, 1863, the regiment participated in the battle of Chackaloo, La., sustaining but small loss.

In April, 1864, the regiment returned to Connecticut on veteran furlough, over 300 of the original men having re-enlisted as veterans. It remained in the State until July 16th, when it proceeded to Bermuda Hundred, Va., where it remained until the 28th of that month. It was then ordered to Deep Bottom, and participated in a demonstration against the enemy.

July 30th it returned to Bermuda Hundred, and embarked for Washington, D. C., arriving there Aug. 1st, and on the following day marched to Tennallytown where it remained until the 14th; on that day it crossed the Potomac and marched via Leesburg to Berrysville, arriving there on the 17th, and from that time participated with the army under the gallant Sheridan in the campaign up the Shenandoah Valley. October 19, 1864, it took an active part in the battle of Cedar Creek, Va., its loss in killed and wounded amounting to 31.

In October the non-veterans of the regiment were mustered out of service, and the remaining veterans were consolidated into a battalion of four companies. The battalion remained in Virginia until Jan. 7, 1865, when it was ordered with its division (the 2d) to Baltimore, Md. It then embarked on the transport "Gen. Sedgwick," and proceeded to Savannah, Ga., where it arrived on the 17th of the same month. The battalion was then engaged in provisional guard duty, and continued in the department of the South until Aug. 3, 1865, when they were mustered out of service.

In every action in which it participated the brave old Ninth made a record worthy of the cause in which it was engaged, and stood by the old flag with heroic devotion.

ITS PRINCIPAL ENGAGEMENTS WERE

Baton Rouge, La., August 5, 1862; *Chackaloo Station, La.,* June 24, 1863; *Deep Bottom, Va.,* July 28, 1864; *Cedar Creek, Va.,* October 19, 1864.

ITS CASUALTIES WERE

Killed in Action,	5
Died of Wounds,	1
Died of Disease,	240
Discharged prior to muster-out,	376
Total,	622

DOW BROTHERS,
Flour Depot,
GROCERY HOUSE,
443 and 447 Main St.,
Under St. John's Hotel,　　HARTFORD.

WE MAKE A SPECIALTY OF

FLOUR!

WHICH WE ARE SELLING AT

Greatly REDUCED PRICES.

SUGARS
OF ALL GRADES SELLING VERY LOW.

OUR
MEAT DEPARTMENT
Is always well stocked with the choicest to be obtained, and selling lower than any other Hartford Market.

Our motto is "Live and Let Live!"

Dow Brothers, under St. John's Hotel.

TENTH REGIMENT INFANTRY.

This regiment left Hartford for Annapolis, Md., October 31, 1861. It was attached to Gen. Burnside's command, and was engaged in the battle of Roanoke Island, Feb. 8, 1862, where it showed sterling bravery. Col. Russell was killed while leading the regiment to a charge.

Lieut.-Col. Drake succeeded to the command of the regiment; he died of disease, June 5, 1862. Col. Pettibone, who succeeded Col. Drake, resigned, and was in turn succeeded by Major Otis as commander.

March 14, 1862, the regiment was again in battle at Newberne, N. C. Again on the 14th of December in the battle of Kingston, N. C., and met with a loss of 100 officers and men; the regiment captured more than fifty of the enemy. December 16th it was engaged in the battle of Whitehall, N. C.

After the battle of Seabrook Island the regiment remained quiet until the siege of Charleston, S. C., from July 28 to Oct. 25, 1863. In December following it took an active part in the battle of St. Augustine, Fla., with a loss of 22 men.

April 18, 1864, it went to Hilton Head, thence by transport to Gloucester, Va., where it was joined by the veterans who had returned from furlough. The camp and garrison equipage, together with the records, were lost by the sinking of a transport that had been stored at Norfolk, and was on its way to the regiment.

May 7th the regiment was in action at Walthall Junction, Va., and from the 13th to the 17th, inclusive, participated in the battle of Drury's Bluff.

Col. Plaisted, Brigade Commander, said as follows: "Of the Tenth Connecticut, I need say no more than that it sustained its splendid reputation. Under a fire in which 18 men fell in as many seconds, not a soldier spoke a word nor moved a heel from the alignment. Too much credit cannot be accorded to Col. Otis for his self-possession under such a fire, and the skillful manner in which he handled his regiment." A detail of the many battles of the Tenth would require a volume of itself.

The regiment continued in service in Virginia until its final muster-out, Aug. 25, 1865, and participated in no less than fourteen engagements between June 16, 1864, and the spring of 1865.

Adjutant-Gen. Williams, in his report dated April 1, 1863, says "that no regiment in the field has seen more active service, better sustained the reputation of Connecticut troops, or met with greater loss than the Tenth."

To say that throughout the whole time it sustained its reputation for bravery and heroic endurance, would be but faint praise for the gallant deeds performed by it.

ITS PRINCIPAL ENGAGEMENTS WERE

Roanoke Island, N. C., Feb. 8, 1862; *Newbernae, N. C.*, March 14, 1862; *Kingston, N. C.*, Dec. 14, 1862; *Whitehall, N. C.*, Dec. 16, 1862; *Seabrook Island, S. C.*, March 28, 1863; *Siege of Charleston, S. C.*, from July 28 to Oct. 25, 1863; *Near St. Augustine, Fla.*, Dec. 30, 1863; *Walthall Junction, Va.*, May 7, 1864; *Drury's Bluff, Va.*, May 13 to 17, 1864, inclusive; *Bermuda Hundred, Va.*, June 16, 1864; *Strawberry Plains, Va.*, July 26 and 27, 1864; *Deep Bottom, Va.*, Aug. 1, 1864; *Deep Bottom, Va.*, Aug. 14, 1864; *Deep Run, Va.*, Aug. 16, 1864; *Siege of Petersburg, Va.*, Aug. 28 to Sept. 29, 1864; *Laurel Hill Church, Va.*, Oct. 1, 1864; *New Market Road, Va.*, Oct. 7, 1864; *Darbytown Road, Va.*, Oct. 13, 1864; *Darbytown Road, Va.*, Oct. 27, 1864; *Johnson's Plantation, Va.*, Oct. 29, 1864; *Hatcher's Run, Va.*, March 29 and 30, and April 1, 1865; *Fort Gregg, Va.*, April 2, 1865; *Appomattox Court House, Va.*, April 9, 1865.

ITS CASUALTIES.

Killed in Action, 57; Died of Wounds, 59; Died of Disease, 152; Discharged prior to muster-out, 692; Total, 960.

DICK WATEROUS,

THE HATTER,

& CO.

Just around the Corner of Main,

AT 13 ASYLUM ST.

ALL KINDS OF

Hats and Caps
CHEAP!

ELEVENTH REGIMENT INFANTRY.

This regiment left Hartford for Annapolis Dec. 16, 1861, under command of Col. Kingsbury. It was assigned to Gen. Burnside's Division, and was called into battle at Newberne, N. C., March 14, 1862, with a loss of six killed. It was attached to the army of the Potomac in July, 1862. Col. Kingsbury resigned March 26th, and Lieut. H. W. Kingsbury, of the U. S. Army, assumed command. It was in the battle of South Mountain, Md., Sept. 14, 1862, and again at Antietam, Sept. 17, 1862, sustaining a loss of 181 killed, wounded, and missing. Col. Kingsbury was among the killed.

Lieut.-Col. Stedman assumed command, and proceeded to Fredericksburg, Va., on the 12th of December, 1862. Being stationed on the picket line it was not actively engaged in the battle of the 13th.

At the siege of Suffolk, from April 11th to May 3d, it was on constant and active duty in the defense of that place. It took part in a reconnoisance under Gen. Corcoran, losing one man killed. On May 4th it was again on a reconnoissance and sustained a loss of four.

Early in March, 1864, the regiment returned from a veteran furlough to Portsmouth, marched to Williamsburg and encamped, and constituted that time the force nearest Richmond on the Peninsula. May 9th it was engaged in the battle of Swift's Creek. On the 16th it participated in the battle of Drury's Bluff, and when under a fearful fire it fell back, with great loss, from a position well nigh fortified with Rebel dead.

June 3d the regiment was engaged in the charge at Cold Harbor, and sustained a loss of 91 officers and men.

On the 5th of August Col. Stedman's brigade was called to the front, and although long unwell from continued exposure in the field the Colonel was in command. He was struck by a random shot in the side, which inflicted a mortal wound, and on the morning of August 6th that most heroic, patriotic, and gallant officer died. Col. Stedman was honored, loved, and respected in life, and sincerely mourned in death.

The regiment continued in active service in front of Petersburg, Va., from June 15, 1864, to August 27, 1864, with a loss of eighty-five officers and men.

From that time until its muster out, Dec. 21, 1865, it continued in service in the Department of Virginia.

No regiment in the service endured with a more heroic valor the hardships of a four years' war than did the ever glorious old Eleventh.

ITS CHIEF ENGAGEMENTS.

Newberne, N. C., March 14, 1862; *South Mountain, Md.*, Sept. 14, 1862; *Antietam, Md.*, Sept. 17, 1862; *Fredericksburg, Va.*, Dec. 12 to 15, 1862; *Suffolk, Va.*, April 24, 1863; *near Suffolk, Va.*, May 4, 1863; *Swift's Creek, Va.*, May 9, 1864; *Drury's Bluffs, Va.*, May 16, 1864; *Cold Harbor, Va.*, June 3, 1864; *before Petersburg, Va.*, June 15 to August 27.

ITS CASUALTIES.

Killed in action,	35	Died of disease, 165
Died of wounds,	41	Discharged prior to muster out, 579
	Total,	820.

TENTING ON THE OLD CAMP GROUND.

We're tenting to-night on the old camp ground,
    Give us a song to cheer
Our weary hearts, a song of home,
    And friends we love so dear.

CHORUS—Many are the hearts that are weary to-night,
        Wishing for the war to cease,
       Many are the hearts looking for the right,
        To see the dawn of peace.
    Tenting to-night, tenting to-night, tenting on the old camp ground.

We've been tenting to-night on the old camp ground,
    Thinking of days gone by,
Of the lov'd ones at home that gave us the hand,
    And the tear that said "Good-bye!"

CHO.—Many are the hearts that are weary to-night,
        Wishing for the war to cease,
       Many are the hearts looking for the right,
        To see the dawn of peace.
    Tenting to-night, tenting to-night, tenting on the old camp ground.

We are tired of war on the old camp ground,
    Many are dead and gone,
Of the brave and true who've left their homes,
    Others been wounded long.

CHO.—Many are the hearts that are weary to-night,
        Wishing for the war to cease,
       Many are the hearts looking for the right,
        To see the dawn of peace.
    Tenting to-night, tenting to-night, tenting on the old camp ground.

We've been fighting to-day on the old camp ground,
    Many are lying near;
Some are dead, and some are dying,
    Many are in tears.

CHO.—Many are the hearts that are weary to-night,
        Wishing for the war to cease,
       Many are the hearts looking for the right,
        To see the dawn of peace.
    Dying to-night, dying to-night, dying on the old camp ground.

TWELFTH REGIMENT INFANTRY.

This splendid regiment, known as the "Charter Oak Regiment," left Hartford under Col. Henry C. Deming, for Ship Island, Feb. 24, 1862, and was attached to Gen. B. F. Butler's division. It was stationed in or near New Orleans during 1862 and part of 1863. On the 31st of January, 1863, Col. Deming resigned, and Lieut.-Col. Colburn was appointed Colonel.

Oct. 27, 1862, it was in the battle of Georgia Landing, La., and lost nineteen men in killed, wounded, and missing.

March 27, 1863, Company A embarked on board the gunboat Diana, with a company of the 160th New York, to make a reconnoissance. Returning through Atchafalaya they were fired upon, and after a severe fight of an hour, were all captured. It is reported they fought with the greatest gallantry, and only surrendered to greatly superior numbers after the boat had been disabled.

On the 9th of April following the regiment started on an expedition against the enemy. On the 13th, at daylight, it formed in support of the 21st Indiana Battery, which opened upon the enemy's fortifications. It shortly afterwards advanced to the front of the enemy's works, and during the day supported several batteries. Companies E, F, and G were advanced as skirmishers. and were actively engaged during the whole of the afternoon. Lieut.-Col. Peck spoke in the highest terms of the conduct of the regiment, and mentions Maj. Lewis and Capts. Brennan and Granuis as deserving of great praise.

The regiment also bore a conspicuous part in the seige of Port Hudson, from May 25 to July 9, 1863, and sustained an aggregate loss of 108 officers and men.

In the spring of 1864 more than three-fourths of the regiment re-enlisted and returned to Connecticut on furlough. On the 8th of May it returned to New Orleans, and remained in that vicinity until July 6, 1864, when it embarked for Fort Monroe, and on August 7th joined the army under General Sheridan, in the Shenandoah Valley. Sept. 19, 1864, it was engaged in the battle of Opequan, Va., losing 71 in killed and wounded. Among the killed were Lieut.-Col. Peck and Lieuts. William S. Buckley and J. W. Steadman. Sept. 22d it was in the battle of Fisher's Hill, sustaining but trifling loss.

Oct. 15th Lieut.-Col. Geo. N. Lewis (promoted from Major vice Peck killed in action), reported for duty, previous to which time he had been absent in Connecticut, from effect of wounds received at Port Hudson, and assumed command.

Oct. 19, 1864, it was in the battle of Cedar Creek, Va , sustaining a loss of 170 officers and men. Capt. Lowell and Lieuts. Phelps and Benton were among the killed.

The severe losses sustained by the command, and the near expiration of their term of service of those who did not re-enlist, necessitated the consolidation of the regiment, and Nov. 26, 1864, it was organized as the Twelfth Battalion Conn. Veteran Vols., and continued to serve in Virginia under Col. Lewis until its muster out, August 12, 1865, leaving behind it a record for bravery, courage, endurance, and discipline, which reflects honor upon the State, whose interests it so gallantly upheld in the field.

ITS GENERAL ENGAGEMENTS.

Georgia Landing, La., Oct. 27, 1862; *Pattersonville, La.*, March 27, 1863; *Bisland, La.*, April 13, 1863; *Siege of Port Hudson, La.*, May 25 to July 9, 1863; *Winchester, Va.*, Sept. 19, 1864; *Fisher's Hill, Va.*, Sept. 22, 1864; *Cedar Creek, Va.*, Oct. 19, 1864.

ITS CASUALTIES.

Killed in action, - - - 50	Died of disease, - - -	188
Died of wounds, - - - 16	Discharged prior to muster out,	501
Total, - - - 755		

THIRTEENTH REGIMENT INFANTRY.

This regiment left New Haven for Ship Island March 17, 1862, 1017 men. All the field officers had seen active service.

It participated in the battle of Georgia Landing, La., Oct. 27, 1862; its loss was not reported.

On the 14th of April, 1863, it took a prominent part in the battle of Irish Bend, La. In this battle the regiment captured a Rebel flag bearing this inscription; "The Ladies of Franklin County to the St. Mary's Cannoniers." The regiment behaved gallantly in this fight, and it was mentioned in official reports as being worthy of special praise for its bravery in its charge upon the enemy's battery. The loss was 53 in killed and wounded.

May 24th following, it was engaged in battle at Port Hudson, and again on the 14th of June was engaged with the enemy at the same place, with a loss of 22 men.

April 11th it embarked with other regiments to join the main army which had met with repulse at Sabine Cross Roads. On the 21st it marched down the river, and on the 22d was engaged in the battle of Cane River, fording the stream in water waist deep, and skirmishing through woods, and over creeks and bluffs, charged the enemy in his entrenchments. It lost at this engagement 3 killed and 21 wounded. The mounted detachment of the 13th suffered severely, 12 out of the 18 present being killed or wounded. On the 16th the enemy was encountered in position at Mansurd Plain, but after a fight of two or three hours he withdrew. This was the last engagement of the 13th in that section. The re-enlisted veterans were furloughed in July, and arrived at Hartford on the 27th.

Aug. 29th it left for Washington, arriving on the 31st, and proceeded to Harper's Ferry, and subsequently joined the army at Berrysville. On Sept. 18th the regiment broke camp, and commenced the advance which, next day, brought on the battle of Winchester, in which it took an active part, sustaining an aggregate loss of 79. Following the routed enemy, he was again confronted at Fisher's Hill. On the morning of the 22d the regiment threw up breastworks, exposed to a murderous fire of the enemy's sharpshooters. At 4 p. m. on the same day an attack was made upon the enemy which was entirely successful, and the 13th was engaged during the night and following day in pursuit of the flying foe.

Oct. 19th it was engaged with the enemy at the battle of Cedar Creek, losing 28 officers and men. On the 23d of Dec. the non-veterans left for New Haven to be mustered-out; the veterans and recruits were consolidated into a battalion, and soon proceeded to Savannah, arriving Jan. 19, 1865. April 25th it was mustered-out at Fort Pulaski, Ga., received their final pay, and was disbanded at Hart's Island, N. Y. harbor, May 4, 1865, having seen more than 3 years' hard service, and achieved a brilliant record.

ITS PRINCIPAL ENGAGEMENTS.

Georgia Landing, La., Oct. 27, 1862; *Irish Bend, La.*, April 14, 1863; *Port Hudson, La.*, May 24, 1863; *Port Hudson, La.*, June 14, 1863; *Cane River, La.*, April 23, 1864; *Mansurd, La.*, May 16, 1864; *Winchester, Va.*, Sept. 19, 1864; *Fisher's Hill, Va.*, Sept. 22, 1864; *Cedar Creek, Va.*, Oct. 19, 1864.

ITS CASUALTIES.

Killed in Action,	32
Died of Wounds,	13
Died of Disease,	129
Discharged prior to muster-out,	705
Total,	879

FOURTEENTH REG'T INFANTRY.

This regiment was the first organized under the call for 300,000 men. It was recruited from the State at large, and left Hartford for Washington Aug. 25, 1862, 1015 men. Without being allowed time for instruction it was ordered forward, and took part in the hard-fought battle of Antietam, meeting with an aggregate loss of 137 men. It was also engaged in the battle of Fredericksburg, sustaining an aggregate loss of 122 men. At this time it had become terribly reduced, numbering scarcely 375 effective men. May 1st, 2d, and 3d it was actively engaged with the enemy at Chancellorville, with a loss of 56. Major Ellis, commanding the regiment, reports that on the morning of the 3d the strength of the command was 219.

It was again engaged at Gettysburg, Pa., July 2d and 3d, and sustained a loss of 66. Major Ellis spoke in the highest terms of the action of the regiment in this battle, mentioning the capture of five regimental battle flags and over 40 prisoners, by a portion of his command which charged the enemy. Four Rebel officers surrendered themselves personally to Major Ellis. This was one of the most trying battles in which the Fourteenth was engaged.

July 14th it was engaged with the enemy at Falling Waters, and again, Oct. 14th, at Auburn, Va. On the latter named day it was also engaged at Bristol Station, losing 26 killed, wounded, and missing.

Oct. 17th it engaged the enemy at Blackburn's Ford, and on the 29th of Nov. following, at Mine Run, losing 14 wounded and captured. On Dec. 2d it returned to its old camp at Mountain Run, accomplishing a march of 45 miles during the 24 hours.

Feb. 6, 1864, it had a hand to hand fight, some of the Fourteenth using its bayonets upon the enemy, and sustaining a loss of 115 in killed, wounded, and missing.

From May, 1864, to Aug. 25th the regiment was engaged in the battles of the Wilderness, Laurel Hill, Spottsylvania, North Anna River, Tolopotomay, Cold Harbor, Petersburg, Deep Bottom, and Ream's Station, Va., and sustained a total of 256 casualties. Col. Ellis reports that both officers and men met fatigue and exposure cheerfully, and bearing without complaint all the hardships they had been called upon to endure.

Oct. 27th the regiment was in action at Boydton Plank Road; total loss, 29. Feb. 5, 1865, it was again in battle at Hatcher's Run, Va., in which Lieut. Bartlett was killed and five men wounded.

As a closing scene in the drama the regiment was present at the battles of High Ridge and Farmville, Va., and was also present at the surrender of the Rebel army under Gen. Lee, thus being permitted to see the desired end accomplished, for which it had so loyally and gloriously struggled.

May 31, 1865, the brave old Fourteenth, numbering 234 officers and men, present and absent, was mustered out of the service, leaving a record of which they may well be proud.

IT TOOK PART IN THE FOLLOWING ENGAGEMENTS:

Antietam, Md., Sept. 17, 1862; Fredericksburg, Va., Dec. 13, 1862; Chancellorsville, Va., May 1st, 2d, and 3d, 1863; Gettysburg, Pa., July 2d and 3d, 1863; Falling Water, Va., July 14, 1863; Auburn, Va., Oct. 14, 1863; Bristol Station, Va., Oct. 14, 1863; Blackburn's Ford, Va., Oct. 17, 1863; Mine Run, Va., Nov. 29, 1863; Morton's Ford, Va., Feb. 6, 1864; Wilderness, Va., May 5 and 6, 1864; Laurel Hill, Va., May 10, 1864; Spottsylvania, Va., May 12, 13, 14, 18, and 22, 1864; North Anna River, Va., May 24 and 26, 1864; Tolopotomay, Va., May 31, 1864; Cold Harbor, Va., June 3 and 6, 1864; Petersburg, Va., June 11 to July 6, 1864; Deep Bottom, Va., Aug. 15 and 16, 1864; Ream's Station, Va., Aug. 25, 1864; Boydton Plank Road, Va., Oct. 27, 1864; Hatcher's Run, Va., Feb. 5, 1865; Hatcher's Run, Va., March 25, 1865; High Bridge, Farmville, Va., and Surrender of Lee's Army, from March 30 to April 10, 1865.

CASUALTIES.

Killed in action, 132; died of wounds, 65; died of disease, 169; discharged prior to muster-out, 416; missing at muster-out of regiment, 6. Total, 788.

HARTFORD SUNDAY JOURNAL,

THE SPICIEST SUNDAY PAPER IN CONNECTICUT.

Established as a Sunday paper April, 1874.   SUBSCRIPTION, $2.50 per year; six months, $1.25.

OFFICE, 284 ASYLUM ST. (Foster Block.)   No Pay No Paper.

G. T. CHAPMAN,
EMPLOYMENT OFFICE,

No. 80½ TRUMBULL STREET,

HARTFORD, CONN.

First-Class Help Furnished for City and Country at Reasonable Rates.

SATISFACTION GUARANTEED.

Veterans of the War for the Union!

LET OLD GLORY WAVE!

While in Hartford on the
BATTLE FLAG GALA DAY!
WILL FIND
"NED" GOGGINS
VETERAN, CO. A,
12th Regiment Conn. Volunteers,
At No. 157 Front St.,
(Cor. Temple,)   HARTFORD,
With a Nice Stock of
Wines, Liquors, Cigars
ETC., ETC.
Give all the Old Boys a Call!

Respectfully, NED GOGGINS, *Veteran, Co. A, 12th C. V.*

FIFTEENTH REG'T INFANTRY.

This regiment was recruited at New Haven, in August, 1862. It left for Washington under command of Col. Dexter R. Wright, Aug. 28, 1862, 1022 officers and men.
Feb. 17, 1863, Col. Wright resigned his position by reason of disability, the command devolving upon Lieut.-Col. Samuel Tolles. Its first general engagement was the battle of Fredericksburg, Dec. 13, 1862, with a total loss of 10.
April 6, 1863, Col. Chas. L. Upham was appointed to the command of the regiment, vice Wright resigned.
During the month of April it was stationed at Suffolk, Va., during the siege by Longstreet, and was engaged in two reconnoisances. In the first, on the Edenton Road, April 24th, it sustained a loss of four. Again on the 3d of May following, it was engaged with the enemy on Providence Church Road, and met with a loss of six killed, wounded, and missing. The regiment was in the expedition of Gen. Dix up the Peninsula, performing some extremely arduous marches. It was engaged during a greater part of the fall and winter in working on the fortifications near Norfolk, Va.
Jan. 24, 1864, it left Portsmouth, Va., for Plymouth, N. C. While there, companies under Major Osborn, with a detachment of the 16th Conn. regiment, were sent on a night expedition to the neighborhood of Colraine, N. C., where they succeeded in destroying a large amount of commissary stores belonging to the enemy. Another force sent out under command of Lieut.-Col. Tolles, attacked the camp of the 62d Georgia regiment, destroying their camp equipage, stores, etc. At the time of the demonstration on Newberne, the regiment was ordered to that place.
March 2, 1865, the regiment joined the forces marching against Goldsboro, N. C. March 7th it was engaged in skirmishing with the enemy at Jackson's Mills, and entrenched themselves during the night within a hundred yards of their works. On the 8th, while briskly engaged, the regiment was enveloped by a division of the enemy, who had gained their rear, and a large portion of the regiment were made prisoners.
Upon the occupation of Kinston by our forces the 15th was left as a part of the garrison, and was assigned to provost duty, which it did until the Rebel armies had surrendered or disbanded, and on June 6th it was ordered to Newberne to prepare for muster-out, which was done June 27, 1865, and it arrived in New Haven July 4th, receiving their final pay July 12, 1865.
Since its organization 595 recruits joined its ranks, making an aggregate of 1617.

ITS ENGAGEMENTS.

Fredericksburg, Va., Dec. 13, 1862; *Edenton Road, Va.*, April 24, 1863; *Providence Church Road, Va.*, May 3, 1863; *Kinston, N. C.*, March 8, 1865.

ITS CASUALTIES.

Killed in Action,	15
Died of Wounds,	15
Died of Disease,	143
Discharged prior to muster-out of regiment,	327
Missing at muster-out of regiment,	57
Total,	557

Gemmill, Burnham & Co.

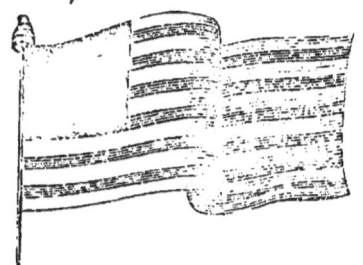

FINE CLOTHING!

VETERANS!

Come in and Look at our New and Beautiful Stock of

FALL CLOTHING!

NOBBY SUITS

Of OUR OWN MAKE at prices that defy competition.

Also a full line of Gent's Furnishing Goods, Underwear, etc.

68 & 70 ASYLUM ST., HARTFORD, CT.

GEMMILL, BURNHAM & CO.

SIXTEENTH REGIMENT INFANTRY.

This regiment was recruited at Hartford, in August, 1862, and left for Washington, D. C., under Col. Frank Beach, on the 29th of the same month. Without having time allowed to learn even the rudiments of military science (many of its members having never loaded a gun), it was hurried forward, and took an active part in the terrible battle of Antietam. Although thus suddenly thrown into the vortex of battle, the men preserved a coolness and displayed a courage highly creditable, as was sufficiently well attested by the severe loss sustained. Among the wounded were Lieut.-Col. Frank Cheney and Major Washburn, both of whom were compelled to resign on account of the severity of their wounds.

Col. Beach, in his report, dated Sept. 19, 1862, remarks that "the enemy commenced shelling us at daylight, and we were kept under a heavy artillery fire at intervals during the day, until about five o'clock, when we were brought against the extreme right of the Rebel infantry, where the battle raged with great fury. That the Sixteenth did nobly is the verdict of all who witnessed its heroism on the battle-field of Antietam." Its aggregate loss in killed and wounded was 185.

The Sixteenth was with the other regiments of the Connecticut Brigade at Suffolk, Va., during the investment of that place by the enemy.

April 24, 1863, the regiment took part in the reconnoissance on the Edenton Road, and after a sharp skirmish with the enemy, the regiment charged and drove the enemy from their pits to their earth-works, and captured several prisoners, with a loss of one killed and seven wounded.

Sunday, May 3, 1863, the regiment was ordered across the Nausemond river, on the Providence Church road, where it was engaged with the enemy several hours. Its loss was two killed and eight wounded. Among the wounded were Capt. Chas. A. Tennant and Sergt. B. F. Blakeslee. Capt. Tennant died of his wounds, and Sergt. Blakeslee was left on the field for dead, having received a serious wound in his head, making the second one in the same place. He was subsequently taken from the field, and recovered to fight in other battles.

June 16, 1863, it moved to Portsmouth, and on the 22d was engaged in the expedition under Gen. Dix, up the Peninsula. The marching was the most severe of any campaign in which it had engaged.

July 14th it returned to Portsmouth, and there remained until January, building fortifications and doing picket duty.

January 21, 1864, the regiment embarked for Plymouth, N. C., and on the 17th of April the enemy attacked Plymouth, and continued the assault until the 20th, when the town and all but one fort of the defenses having fallen into the hands of the enemy, the place was surrendered. Nearly the whole regiment was captured, and many of its members perished in the Rebel prisons of Andersonville and Florence. Company H was not with the regiment at the surrender of Plymouth, and consequently escaped capture. This company, with about 25 other members of the regiment, were stationed at Roanoke Island, where they remained until March 4, 1865, when they were ordered to Newberne, N. C., and June 24, 1865, the Sixteenth was mustered out of the service of the United States.

The colors of the regiment were torn from their standards at the capture of Plymouth, to prevent their falling into the hands of the enemy. Some few pieces were saved by its members, who concealed them about their persons, carried them through their prison life, and brought them safely home. They have been put together as best they could be, and will attract attention on Battle Flag Day and at the Capitol. The remainder of the colors were burned.

Col. Burnham, in his report, dated the 10th of August, 1864, said, "While I have reason to express my satisfaction with the conduct of my entire command, I deem it but just to mention Capt. Thos. F. Burke, Lieut. Landon, and Lieut. John B. Clapp, my adjutant, as coming under my immediate observation in the performance of especial gallantry."

The regiment went out 1000 strong, and returned home 135 officers and men, which we believe to be the smallest number of any regiment that returned to the State.

ITS ENGAGEMENTS.

Antietam, Md., Sept. 17, 1862; loss in killed, 5 officers, 38 men; wounded, 8 officers, 134 men; total loss, 185; *Fredericksburg, Va.*, Dec. 12, 13, and 14, 1862; *Edenton Road, Va.*, April 24, 1863; *Providence Church Road, Va.*, May 3, 1864; *Plymouth, N. C.*, April 20, 1864.

CASUALTIES.

Killed in action,	46
Died of wounds,	24
Died of disease,	224
Discharged prior to muster out of regiment,	336
Missing at muster out of regiment,	27
Total,	707

THE BATTLE FLAG RE-UNION!

SOLDIERS OF THE LATE WAR

Visiting Hartford Sept. 17, will find a quiet and cosy place to get a square Lunch with all the et ceteras, cheap and nice, at

M. H. WELCH'S RESTAURANT,

127 Main Street.

Respectfully, M. H. WELCH, Co. F, 16th Reg't. Conn. Vols.

SEVENTEENTH REG'T INFANTRY.

This regiment was organized in August, 1862, and left for Washington September 3, 1862, under command of Col. Wm. H. Noble, and was attached to the Army of the Potomac.

May 2, 1863, it participated in the battle of Chancellorsville, Va., and fully sustained the reputation of Connecticut troops for bravery and endurance, as is clearly exhibited in the long list of casualties. During the battle it was called upon to use the bayonet, and although driven from positions at different times while the fight was in progress, it is clearly set forth in the several official reports that had all performed their duty with the same degree of bravery and fidelity exhibited by the 17th, the result would have been less disastrous. Its loss was 120 men killed, wounded, and missing.

July 1st to 4th it was engaged in the battle of Gettysburg, and again was it called upon to give up some of its bravest and best, its aggregate loss being 198 killed, wounded, and missing.

After a year's service in the Army of the Potomac, it was, in Aug. 1863, transferred to the Department of the South, and located at Folly Island. It was subsequently ordered to St. Augustine, Florida, and relieved the 10th Connecticut.

May 19th, Company B, which composed the picket posts at Welaka and Saunders, on the St. John river, was captured by the Rebels.

Lieut.-Col. Wilcoxson started from St. Augustine. Feb. 3, 1865, upon an expedition for the purpose of procuring some cotton belonging to a Rebel Colonel, which was stored near Dunn's Lake, nearly 75 miles distant; he succeeded in capturing the cotton, but after marching some seven miles upon his return, was attacked, wounded, and was taken prisoner with his command; the loss was 36 in killed, wounded, and captured. The detachment was so suddenly attacked by such an overwhelming force that it could make but little show of resistance. Major Allen in his report remarks, "The brave young Chatfield fell, shot through and through the body. He was in the act of cutting his way through the Rebels when he received his mortal wound. He died as he had lived—a courageous soldier, and an honor to our State and country."

June 19, 1865, it was ordered to Jacksonville to await the arrival of detached companies, when it was to proceed to Hilton Head, S. C., for muster-out, which occurred July 9, 1865.

Thus ended the service of a regiment which, for courage and endurance, had no superior in the field.

ITS ENGAGEMENTS.

Chancellorsville, Va., May 2, 1863. Total loss, 120.
Gettysburg, Pa., July 1, 2, 3, and 4, 1863. Total loss, 198.
Welaka and Saunders, Fla., May 19, 1864. Total loss, 40.
Dunn's Lake, Fla., Feb. 5, 1865. Total loss, 36.

ITS CASUALTIES.

Killed in action,	29
Died of wounds,	15
Died of disease,	74
Discharged prior to muster-out of regiment,	319
Missing at muster-out of regiment,	9
Total,	446

TEA IMPORTERS.

THE GREAT
Atlantic and Pacific
TEA COMPANY

429 Main St.,

THE LARGEST AND CHEAPEST TEA COMPANY

IN THE WORLD.

THE ONLY IMPORTERS AND RETAILERS IN THE UNITED STATES.

WE PRESENT TO EVERY PURCHASER OF

$3.00, $5.00, AND $8.00 WORTH OF

TEA AND COFFEE

ONE OF OUR

BEAUTIFUL OIL CHROMOS,

HANDSOMELY FRAMED IN GOLD OR BLACK WALNUT.

WE GUARANTEE OUR TEAS AND COFFEES
25 PER CENT. CHEAPER THAN ANY HOUSE IN THE UNITED STATES.

LIBERAL Discount and Express paid on all orders of twenty pounds and upwards.

W. BROOKES, Manager,
429 MAIN ST., HARTFORD, CONN.

EIGHTEENTH REG'T INFANTRY.

The 18th regiment was organized in August, and left Norwich for Washington Aug. 22, 1862, and was assigned to the Army of the Potomac.

It performed guard duty at Baltimore until May 22, 1863, when it was ordered to the district of West Virginia.

June 13th, 14th, and 15th, it took an active part in the battle of Winchester, Va., and a large proportion of its officers and men were taken prisoners.

During the night of the 15th the order was given for the silent evacuation of Winchester. The 1st and 2d brigades commenced the retreat under cover of the darkness, but were intercepted by a superior force of the enemy and at once became engaged; after two charges by the brigades they were so badly broken that re-organization was impracticable. The 18th was reformed with some difficulty and charged the third time alone, but was immediately repulsed, with a loss of 30 killed and wounded. Major Peale with about 30 men succeeded in making their escape in a body. Company D alone escaped intact, having left Winchester in charge of some prisoners. The total loss in this engagement was 587, in killed, wounded, and captured. The captured were soon exchanged and returned to the regiment then near Harper's Ferry.

May 15, 1864, it was in the engagement with the enemy at New Market, Va., but was compelled to retreat owing to the superior strength of the enemy. It sustained a total loss of 56 in killed, wounded, and missing.

June 5th it was in the battle of Piedmont, Va. Major Peale reports that on nearing the main line of the enemy, the regiment was subjected to continuous volleys of musketry, which though considerably depleting their ranks did not cause their line to waver in the least. After hours of severe fighting the enemy was totally routed and nearly 1500 of their number captured, not including the wounded. Its total loss in killed and wounded was 122.

June 18th the regiment again encountered the enemy at Lynchburg, Va., sustaining a loss of 9 men. The command was compelled to fall back, closely followed by the enemy's cavalry. They were almost constantly on the march until July 3d, when they arrived at Camp Piatt, West Va. On this march the sufferings of the men were intense; many having fallen from exhaustion and hunger were taken prisoners.

July 18, 1864, it participated in an engagement with the Rebels that invaded Maryland and Pennsylvania during the early part of July, in which it acted well its part and suffered severely, sustaining a loss of 32 killed and wounded.

July 24th it was engaged with the enemy at Winchester, Va.

Sept. 3, 1864, it was in action at Berryville, Va., fortunately with small loss. It continued to serve in the district of West Va. until its final muster-out, June 27, 1865, at Harper's Ferry.

ITS ENGAGEMENTS.

Winchester, Va., June 13, 14, and 15, 1863; *New Market, Va.*, May 15, 1864; *Piedmont, Va.*, June 5, 1864; *Lynchburg, Va.*, June 18, 1864; *Snicker's Ford, Va.*, July 18, 1864; *Winchester, Va.*, July 24, 1864; *Berryville, Va.*, Sept. 3, 1864.

CASUALTIES.

Killed in action, 52; died of wounds, 14; died of disease, 72; discharged prior to muster-out of regiment, 323; missing at muster-out of regiment, 12; Total, 473.

ALL THE VETERANS

And all the Patriotic People visiting the Capitol City on the

GREAT BATTLE FLAG DAY!

AND AT ALL OTHER TIMES, WILL FIND US ON HAND WITH THE

LARGEST AND FINEST STOCK OF

TO BE FOUND IN CONNECTICUT.

DROP IN AT THE POPULAR

BOOT AND SHOE EMPORIUM.

It will do you good to look over the stock and store, if you do not purchase.

D. A. STRONG,

No. 483 MAIN STREET,

(CHENEY BUILDING,)

HARTFORD, CONN.

TWENTIETH REGIMENT.

This regiment left New Haven for Washington Sept. 11, 1862, under command of Col. Samuel Ross, and was assigned to the Army of the Potomac.

May 1st, 2d, and 3d it was engaged in the battle of Chancellorsville, behaving most gallantly during the engagement, and was highly complimented for its bravery. Its total loss was 197 men, killed, wounded, and missing.

July 2 and 3. 1863, it participated in the battle of Gettysburg, occupying the right of the line. On the night of the 2d it lay in line of battle in a cornfield, ready at a moment's notice. On the morning of the 3d a portion of the regiment was thrown forward as skirmishers, the whole regiment being hotly engaged with the enemy, and was constantly under arms during the nights of the 3d and 4th. Col. Wooster said, "Each officer and man then with me seemed intent only on doing his whole duty, cheerfully and promptly executing every order." Total loss in this engagement, 28.

In September, 1863, it was transferred to the Army of the Cumberland. It arrived at Bridgeport, Ala., Oct. 3d. It participated in several skirmishes with the enemy during the autumn months. Jan. 20, 1864, while a portion of the regiment was guarding Tracy City, Tenn., the place was attacked by Rebel cavalry, who were repulsed and forced to retreat.

May 15, 1864, it took part in the battle of Resaca, Ga., and on the 19th it was engaged with the enemy at Cassville, Ga.; the aggregate loss in the two engagements being 21 killed and wounded.

It continued its march with Sherman's army, and on July 20th participated in the battle of Peach Tree Creek, Ga., which was one of unusual severity, the total loss being 55 in killed and wounded.

Again, on the 21st of July, the regiment was engaged with the enemy near Atlanta, with a loss of 10 men.

On the 25th of August it marched to Turner's Ferry, and on the 27th it was engaged in a skirmish with the enemy. Sept. 2d it participated in the capture of Atlanta. It arrived at Savannah, Ga., Dec. 10th. It was engaged in various siege operations against that place until the 21st, when the enemy having evacuated, it entered the city.

March 15, 1865, it encountered the enemy at Silver Run, N. C., and after a short engagement, drove them from their line of works, its loss being 19 in killed and wounded.

On the 19th of the same month it participated in the battle of Bentonville, and fully sustained its courage and valor, which it had already established on many a hard fought battle-field.

During the campaign the regiment marched more than 500 miles, endured wet, cold, hunger, and fatigue without a murmur, and was finally mustered out of service, June 13, 1865, numbering 506, present and absent.

ITS ENGAGEMENTS.

Chancellorsville, Va., May 3, 1863; *Gettysburg, Pa.*, July 2 and 3, 1863; *Tracy City, Tenn.*, Jan. 20, 1863; *Resaca, Ga.*, May 15, 1864; *Cassville, Ga.*, May 19, 1864; *Peach Tree Creek, Ga.*, July 20, 1864; *near Atlanta, Ga.*, Aug. 7, 1864; *Silver Run, N. C.*, March 15, 1865; *Bentonville, N. C.*, March 19, 1865; *Raleigh, N. C.*, April 13, 1865.

CASUALTIES.

Killed in action,	50
Died of wounds,	37
Died of disease,	77
Discharged prior to muster out of regiment,	264
Missing at muster out of regiment,	2
Total,	430

T. F. BURKE,

MANUFACTURER OF
MIRROR, PORTRAIT,
PICTURE FRAMES,
AND WINDOW CORNICES.

Old Frames Re-Gilt,   Furniture Gilded,
OIL PAINTINGS CLEANED, VARNISHED, AND REPAIRED.

N. B.—Work done for the Trade.

162 ASYLUM STREET.

THE BATTLE FLAG JUBILEE,
SEPT. 17, 1879.

When you visit the Capitol on that day, or at any time, drop in at the

CITY HOTEL
Billiard Parlors

if you would enjoy a game of Billiards on tables of the most approved make.

All its surroundings First-class.

"ELECK" BOWERS, Manager.

GEORGE F. ALLEN'S
Board and Feeding Stables,
328 ASYLUM ST.,

(Few Rods East of Depot,)   HARTFORD, CONN.

LIGHT, AIRY, NEAT, AND CONVENIENT.

Second to none in the City.   *Terms most Reasonable.*

TWENTY-FIRST REGIMENT.

This regiment was organized in August, 1862, Col. Arthur Dutton commanding. It left Norwich for the seat of war Sept. 11, 1862, and was assigned to the Army of the Potomac.

Its first engagement was at the battle of Fredericksburg, Dec. 13, 1862, where it sustained a loss of six men wounded. Col. Dutton spoke in the highest terms of the conduct of the regiment in this, its first battle.

In the months of April and May, 1863, it participated in the defense of Suffolk, Va., and engaged the enemy on the Edenton road, meeting with a small loss.

May 2d it was ordered to cross the Nansemond river at Sleepy Hole, to seize Reed's Ferry, and open communication with the Fourth Rhode Island regiment on the left. Gen. Getty, in his report, said: "I cannot suffer to pass unnoticed the services of those who crossed the Nansemond at Sleepy Hole, who drove the enemy's cavalry from Chuckatuc, and seized Reed's Ferry, capturing several prisoners. Such deeds prove the mettle of the men."

Shortly afterwards it was transferred to the Department of Virginia and North Carolina, and was subsequently ordered to Newport News, where it remained nearly six weeks. Feb. 3, 1864, it was ordered to Morehead City, N. C., and after aiding in repelling the enemy at that point, it was sent to Newberne, N. C.

May 16, 1864, the regiment took an active part in the battle of Drury's Bluff, Va., and sustained a loss of 107 killed, wounded, and missing, which fully attests to the fact that brave men were in its ranks, and bravely fighting they fell.

May 25th it was ordered to reconnoiter the enemy's left, but night coming on they returned to camp. The day following it again moved, with orders to push the reconnoissance until stopped by the enemy. After an advance of nearly two miles the enemy was found strongly entrenched. Line of battle was formed, and the skirmishers were becoming engaged, when Col. Dutton was mortally wounded. The command devolved on Lieut.-Col. Burpee, who was finally obliged to withdraw his command.

June 3, 1864, the regiment was in the battle of Cold Harbor, Va., receiving well-merited compliments from division and brigade commanders. It sustained a loss of 47 men.

It remained in front of Petersburg until Sept. 3d, performing picket duty and engaged in skirmishes with the enemy. Its loss while thus engaged was 49 men.

Sept. 28th it marched to the James river, crossed on pontoon bridges, and proceeded to the assault on Fort Harrison, and on the day following (29th) the fort, with its garrison and armament of twenty-two pieces of heavy ordnance, fell into the hands of the Union forces. The fighting was extremely severe, but the Twenty-first did not fail to add new laurels to its wreath. This was the last general engagement of the regiment. Nothing of importance occurred subsequently, and the Twenty-first was mustered out of the service on the 16th day of June, 1865, leaving a decidedly brilliant record.

ITS ENGAGEMENTS.

Fredericksburg, Va., Dec. 13, 1862; *Suffolk, Va.,* April and May, 1863; *Drury's Bluffs, Va.,* May 16, 1864; *Cold Harbor, Va.,* June 3, 1864; *before Petersburg, Va.,* May 26 to June 19, 1864; *before Petersburg, Va.,* June 19 to Sept. 3, 1864; *Fort Harrison, Va.,* Sept. 29 to Oct. 1, 1864.

CASUALTIES.

Killed in action, 26; died of wounds, 33; died of disease, 108; discharged prior to muster out of regiment, 313; missing at time of muster out of regiment, 2. Total, 482.

TWENTY-SECOND REG'T (9 Months).

This regiment was organized in 1862. It received marching orders October 7, 1862, and proceeded to Washington, was assigned to the Army of the Potomac, and during the Winter was stationed at Miner's Hill, Va., near Washington. The regiment was recruited for nine months' service.

April 15, 1863, the regiment broke camp and marched to Alexandria, and embarked for Fortress Monroe; from thence to Suffolk, Va., at that time besieged by Gen. Longstreet, of the Rebel forces. In the battle of May 3d, across the Nansemond, it supported the Eighth Conn. and the Eighty-Ninth New York, being ordered out at midnight and constantly under fire.

After the retreat of Longstreet it was ordered with the division to West Point, Va., but on the defeat of Gen. Hooker, were hastily ordered back to Yorktown; from thence it proceeded to Diascomb Bridge, within twenty miles of Richmond. Its term of service having expired it returned to Hartford, and was mustered out July 7, 1863.

This regiment was composed of excellent material, was commanded by Col. Geo. S. Burnham, an experienced officer, formerly Col. of the 1st Connecticut regiment (three months), and, had the opportunity been granted it, none can doubt but that it would have won for itself a brilliant record on the field of battle.

ITS CASUALTIES.

Died of disease,	20
Discharged prior to muster-out of regiment,	77
Total,	97

TWENTY-THIRD REGIMENT (9 Months).

The 23d regiment was organized in September, 1862, and rendezvoused at Camp Terry, New Haven. It received marching orders Nov. 16, 1862, and proceeded to Camp Buckingham, L. I., where it remained until the following month, when it was assigned to Banks' expedition, and embarked on transports for New Orleans.

The regiment was for most of the time engaged in guarding the New Orleans & Opelousas Railroad.

On the 2d of June, while the greater part of Gen. Banks' army was before Port Hudson, the Rebels made an attack upon the line of the road and succeeded in capturing or destroying a large amount of stores at Brashear City. A number of officers of the regiment who were on duty at that place were captured.

It bore an honorable part in repelling several attacks on the road, but no official report of engagements was received by the Adjutant-General, consequently no detailed account of its history can be given.

It returned to New Haven on the expiration of its term of service, and was mustered out Aug. 31, 1863.

ITS CASUALTIES.

Killed, 3; died of wounds, 4; died of disease, 44; discharged prior to muster-out of regiment, 21. Total, 72.

TWENTY-FOURTH REGIMENT.

The Twenty-fourth Regiment was organized in September, 1862. Six companies of this regiment were recruited in Middlesex county, and the four others (three of them Irish) from Hartford, New Haven, and Fairfield counties. Col. Samuel M. Marsfield, a Lieutenant in the regular army, was appointed to the command.

This regiment was also assigned to Gen. Banks' expedition, and left its rendezvous at Middletown, Conn., Nov. 18, 1862, with 698 officers and men, for Camp Buckingham, L. I., from whence it proceeded to New Orleans, and from thence to Baton Rouge, La. Soon after it was ordered to join the army before Port Hudson. The following is a summary of its operations :

May 21, 1863, it was landed from transports, and marched to rear of Port Hudson. May 24th it was engaged with the enemy, whom they drove from their rifle pits, and held the border of the woods, within a few yards of the enemy's breast-works, until next morning, when it was relieved, and five companies were sent further to the right as skirmishers. May 27, 1863, the skirmishers were called in, and the regiment moved to support Gen. Weitzel's storming columns ; and on the 31st it was detailed to support batteries on the right.

June 1st it was before Port Hudson, with the reserve of the right wing, until the morning of the 14th, the day of the second assault on Port Hudson, in which the regiment played a conspicuous part. It advanced further to the front, in face of a most galling fire, and held the advanced position for the rest of the month, one-half of the regiment on duty day and night.

July 1, 1863, the regiment was in trenches before the enemy, and was under a brisk fire until the surrender, which took place on the 8th of July.

July 11th it entered the fortress, and embarked on transports to Danielsonville, and from thence to Carrolton. The loss of the regiment during the siege was quite severe.

The regiment served in the Department of the Gulf nearly ten and a half months, and was finally mustered out of service Sept. 30, 1863 with a most honorable record.

ITS ENGAGEMENTS.

Port Hudson, La., from May 23 to July 11, 1863. Loss in killed, 14 enlisted men; wounded, 6 commissioned officers, 46 enlisted men. Total loss, 66.

CASUALTIES.

Killed in action,	14
Died of wounds,	4
Died of disease,	47
Discharged prior to muster out of regiment,	38
Total,	103

TRAMP! TRAMP! TRAMP!

(THE PRISONER'S HOPE.)

In the prison cell I sit, thinking, mother dear, of you,
    And our bright and happy home so far away,
And the tears they fill my eyes, spite of all that I can do,
    Though I try to cheer my comrades and be gay.

Chorus.

Tramp, tramp, tramp, the boys are marching,
    Cheer up, comrades, they will come,
And beneath the starry flag we shall breathe the air again,
    Of the free-land in our own beloved home.

In the battle front we stood when the fiercest charge they made,
    And they swept us off a hundred men or more,
But before we reached their lines they were beaten back dismayed,
    And we heard the cry of vict'ry o'er and o'er.

Chorus.

Tramp, tramp, tramp, the boys are marching, etc.

So within the prison cell we are waiting for the day
    That shall come to open wide the iron door,
And the hollow eye grows bright, and the poor heart almost gay,
    As we think of seeing home and friends once more.

Chorus.

Tramp, tramp, tramp, the boys are marching, etc.

TWENTY-FIFTH REGIMENT.

This regiment rendezvoused at Camp Halleck, Hartford, and left for Camp Buckingham, Centerville, L. I., Nov. 14, 1862, Col. Geo. P. Bissell commanding. It formed a part of Gen. Banks' division, and after a short stay at Centerville, embarked for New Orleans. No official report of its movements prior to the month of March, 1863, were received.

March 13th the regiment advanced toward Port Hudson. That night it bivouacked about eight miles from Baton Rouge. On the 14th it advanced some five miles further and then took a position near the enemy's works. The object of the expedition (attracting the attention of the enemy while the Union fleet passed the batteries, and the marking of a movement on the Clinton road by another portion of the army) having been accomplished, the entire army fell back in a most severe storm, which, while it seriously affected the comfort of our forces, frustrated the design of the enemy to attack the Union column.

The sufferings of the 25th were reported to be almost unendurable.

March 9, 1863, the regiment marched to Brashear City, where it remained until the 12th, when it commenced skirmishing with the enemy. On the 16th it was thrown to the front and right to skirmish and cover the advance of the main body, and shortly after began the battle of Irish Bend, in which the regiment took an active part, acquitting itself in a most noble manner, and meeting with a total loss of 96, while only *one* of the whole was reported missing, all the others being killed or wounded. The regiment was commanded by Col. Bissell in person.

From the date of the battle of Irish Bend until May 25th, the regiment was engaged in marches, and was for the most part without communication with its baggage; at one time officers and men being without a change of clothing for a month.

May 24th commenced the investment of the works before Port Hudson, this regiment being assigned the center. The regiment was under command of Major McManus during the battle, Col. Bissell being absent, sick.

That the regiment bore a conspicuous part in this battle is fully attested in the official reports. Some of its men were without rations for some forty hours, and yet they performed their duties without a murmur. It sustained an aggregate loss of 28 officers and men.

Again, on the 14th and 15th of June, it participated in another attack on the enemy's works, and sustained a loss of 18 killed and wounded. After such a long and tedious campaign the regiment became greatly reduced, and on the morning of the 26th of June Adjutant Ward reported but one hundred and forty men fit for duty.

By the bravery displayed on the field of battle, and the patient endurance on the many long marches, the regiment won for itself a high and lasting reputation. It continued in active service in the Department of the Gulf until the expiration of its term of service, and was mustered out Aug. 26, 1863.

ITS PRINCIPAL ENGAGEMENTS.

Irish Bend, La., April 14, 1863.
Port Hudson, La., May 25 and 26, 1863.
Port Hudson, La., June 14 and 15, 1863.

ITS CASUALTIES.

Killed in action,	14
Died of wounds,	13
Died of disease,	56
Discharged prior to muster-out of regiment,	60
Total,	143

TWENTY-SIXTH REGIMENT.

This regiment was recruited in New London and Windham counties, and rendezvoused at Camp Russell, Norwich. It was commanded by Col. Thomas G. Kingsley, and left the State for Camp Buckingham, Centerville, L. I., Nov. 13, 1862, and was attached to Gen. Banks' Army Corps.

Its first general engagement was May 27, 1863, in an assault upon Port Hudson, in which it bore a conspicuous part, and distinguished itself by its energetic action. The regiment occupied the third line in the assault, and was exposed to a murderous fire of shell, shot, grape, and canister, and after an hour's severe fighting the men were compelled to seek shelter behind stumps and logs. Col. Kingsley was wounded in the engagement. Its total loss was 107 in killed, wounded, and missing.

June 13th the regiment, commanded by Lieut.-Col. Selden, participated in a skirmish before Port Hudson, and sustained a loss of eight men in killed and wounded.

Again, on the 14th, it was engaged with the enemy before Port Hudson, and sustained a loss of 59 men killed and wounded.

The records show that when the Twenty-sixth came out of the assault its loss was nearly one-half of the entire brigade. It took into action 235 officers and men, none of whom faltered, but each doing all that was required of him in a heroic manner. That it distinguished itself for bravery, fidelity, and endurance during the entire siege, is conceded by all who witnessed its gallant deeds.

The official reports received from the regiment were very meager, giving only the casualties; consequently a more detailed summary of its services cannot be given.

The regiment returned to Connecticut, and was mustered out of service at Norwich, Aug. 17, 1863.

ITS GENERAL ENGAGEMENTS.

Port Hudson, La., May 27, 1863; *Port Hudson, La.*, June 13 and 14, 1863.

CASUALTIES.

Killed in action,	15
Died of wounds,	30
Died of disease,	72
Discharge prior to muster out of regiment,	52
Total,	169

TWENTY-SEVENTH REGIMENT.

This regiment was organized in Sept., 1862, and was recruited wholly from New Haven county. It was commanded by Col. Richard L. Bostwick. It received marching orders Oct. 22, 1862, left its camp at New Haven, and proceeded to Washington with 820 men.

It was assigned to the army of the Potomac, and on the 13th of December, 1862, participated in the battle of Fredericksburg. Fortunately, a portion of the command had been detailed for picket duty at Falmouth, and were not relieved in time to participate in the battle with the regiment, otherwise its loss would have been much more severe. Col. Bostwick, in his report of the battle, said: "Without any attempt to flatter a regiment which I had the honor to command, I can justly say that both officers and men behaved exceedingly well; doing nobly, without flinching, under a severe and galling fire from the enemy, of which the killed and wounded is a criterion." The regiment sustained a total loss of 105 killed, wounded, and missing.

After the battle of Fredericksburg the regiment was engaged in the usual picket duty and skirmishing incident to army life, and on May 3, 1863, it was engaged in the sanguinary battle of Chancellorsville, Va., sustaining an aggregate loss of 202 men, most of whom were captured. The captured were soon exchanged, and the regiment continued its active life on picket and in the skirmish until the 1st of July, when it proceeded to Gettysburg, Pa., and on the 2d and 3d it was engaged in the great battle at that place. Its aggregate loss in that engagement was 39 killed, wounded, and missing.

We quote: "It is to be regretted that no reports of the part taken by the regiment in the last two battles were ever received by the Adjutant-General."

The regiment was mustered out at New Haven July 27, 1863, upon the expiration of its term of service.

Col. Brooks said: "Side by side with the veterans of the army of the Potomac it has fought, and by the gallantry of its conduct won for itself an enviable name and reputation, and which may well in after years cause all who belong to the 27th to point to their record with pride."

ITS ENGAGEMENTS.

Fredericksburg, Va., Dec. 13, 1862; *Chancellorsville, Va.*, May 8, 1863; *Gettysburg, Pa.*, July 2 and 3, 1863.

CASUALTIES.

Killed in action,	28
Died of wounds,	17
Died of disease,	22
Discharged prior to muster out of regiment,	82
Total,	149

R. P. KENYON & CO.,

23 Asylum St., Hartford, Conn.,

Are prepared for the Great Crowd visiting Hartford on

THE GREAT BATTLE FLAG DAY!

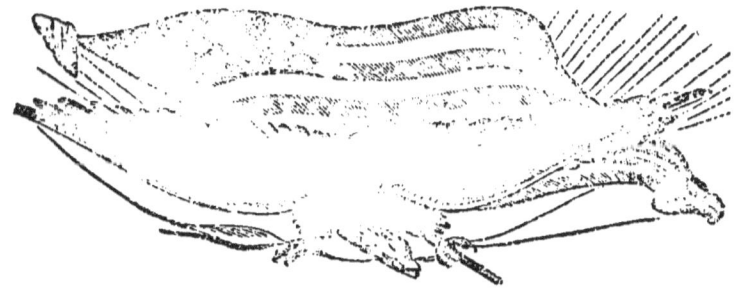

With a Large and Magnificent Stock of

HATS & CAPS,

TRUNKS, BAGS, etc.

23 Asylum St. is the place for Bargains.

"Just the 2d Hat Store around the Corner."

R. P. KENYON & CO.

The only Wholesale Jobbing Hat House in the State of Connecticut.

TWENTY-EIGHTH REGIMENT.

The Twenty-eighth regiment was composed of eight companies, recruited in Litchfield and Fairfield counties, and numbered 678 men.

It went into camp at New Haven, where it remained until it received marching orders, Nov. 18, 1862. This regiment was also assigned to Gen. Banks' army corps, making the fifth furnished by Connecticut for this expedition. Col. Samuel P. Ferris, its commander, was appointed from the regular army.

During the early part of its services the regiment was reported at Pensacola, Fla. Soon after it received marching orders, joined the army moving upon Port Hudson, and was actively engaged in the assault on that place June 14, 1863. It sustained a loss of 59 in killed and wounded. Among the former were two commissioned officers, Capt. David D. Hoag and Lieut. Charles Durand. No official reports were received by the Adjutant-General, and it is therefore impossible to give a detailed account of its service. The only list of casualties received was contained in the monthly return of June, 1863.

The regiment was present at the fall of Port Hudson, and was ordered inside the works, and formed a part of the garrison until relieved and ordered home.

It was mustered out of the service at New Haven, Conn., Aug. 28, 1863.

It took a part in the following engagement:

Port Hudson, La., June 14, 1863.

CASUALTIES.

Killed in action,	9
Died of wounds,	9
Died of disease,	65
Discharged prior to muster out of regiment,	14
Total,	97

Z. C. ALDEN'S
CATARRH CURE.
AN ENTIRELY VEGETABLE COMPOUND.

Cures all Head and Throat Diseases, Headache, Rumbling Noises in the Head, Deafness, Dizziness, Coughing and Vomiting in the morning, Hacking, Tickling Coughs, which is always attended with Catarrh; cures Dryness and Inflammation in the Nose and Throat.

It can be used as a SNUFF, or made into a LIQUID by dissolving in water, according to Directions around each bottle.

A CERTAIN CURE IS GUARANTEED.

Prepared by Z. C. ALDEN, HARTFORD, CONN.

WHOLESALE AGENTS—JOHN F. HENRY & CO., No. 8 College Place, New York.
GEORGE C. GOODWIN & CO., 33 Hanover Street, Boston.

ASK YOUR DRUGGIST FOR IT.

JUST BEFORE THE BATTLE, MOTHER.

Just before the battle, mother,
  I am thinking most of you,
While upon the field we're watching,
  With the enemy in view.
Comrades brave are round me lying,
  Fill'd with thoughts of home and God,
For well they know that on the morrow
  Some will sleep beneath the sod.

Chorus.
Farewell, mother, you may never
  Press me to your heart again;
O, you'll not forget me, mother,
  If I'm numbered with the slain.

Oh! I long to see you, mother,
  And the loving ones at home,
But I'll never leave our banner,
  Till in honor I can come.
Tell the traitors all around you,
  That their cruel words we know
In every battle kill our soldiers,
  By the help they give the foe.

Chorus—Farewell, mother, etc.

Hark! I hear the bugle sounding,
  'Tis the signal for the fight;
Now may God protect us, mother,
  As he ever does the right.
Hear the battle-cry of Freedom,
  How it swells upon the air,
Yes! we'll rally round the standard,
  Or we'll perish nobly there.

Chorus—Farewell, mother, etc.

TWENTY-NINTH REGIMENT (Colored).

Recruiting for this regiment commenced early in the fall of 1863, and by the latter part of January, 1864, the maximum number had been enlisted. During its organization the regiment was stationed at Fair Haven, Conn. It was formally mustered into the service of the United States on the 8th of March, 1864. On the 12th of March Col. Wm. B. Wooster, formerly of the 20th Connecticut Volunteers, reported to the regiment and soon after assumed command. On the 20th of March it left New Haven harbor on transport, and after a pleasant passage disembarked at Annapolis, Md.

The regiment up to this time had been unarmed, but was supplied with a full complement of the best Springfield rifle muskets. It was assigned to the 9th Corps, then assembling at Annapolis, and on the 9th of April left Annapolis for Hilton Head, S. C., thence to Beaufort, S. C., where it disembarked on the 13th. After receiving a few months' instructions the regiment was ordered to Virginia, and on the 8th of August left Beaufort for Bermuda Hundred, Va., where it disembarked on the 14th of the same month. It was immediately ordered out on reconnoissance and is reported to have acted in this, its first engagement, in the most gallant manner.

August 24th the 10th Corps, to which the regiment was attached, relieved the 18th Corps in front of Petersburg, and the regiment continued in the trenches until Sept. 24th, when it was ordered to the rear for rest and the replenishing of its scanty wardrobe, the men being ragged and barefoot. After a few days of rest it was again on the war-path, and was continually engaged in reconnoisances and skirmishes until the 19th of November, when it was ordered to garrison certain detached forts on the New Market Road, which was considered of great importance on account of their relation to the whole line North of the James. That this regiment was sent to hold them was a fitting tribute to its valor and efficiency.

There it remained until Dec. 8th, when it removed to the left of Fort Harrison. It continued in this position during the balance of the Winter, picketing, drilling, building forts, and making roads preparatory to the Spring campaign.

Prior to March, 1865, the regiment had sustained a loss of 143 in killed, wounded, and missing.

In March the regiment was stationed at Fort Harrison, one of the most important positions in the whole line. On Saturday and Sunday, April 1st and 2d, the fighting on the left had been terrific and generally in favor of the Union troops. The regiment was ordered to observe with great care the movements of the enemy in its immediate front, and on Saturday, the 2d of April, witnessed the last Rebel dress parade in Virginia. Early on Monday, April 3d, the picket fires of the enemy began to wane, and an ominous silence prevailed within the lines; in a short time deserters began to come within the Union lines, and in a little while the regiment witnessed the barracks of Fort Darling in flames, while tremendous explosions followed each other in rapid succession. The early dawn revealed the deserted lines of the enemy, with guns spiked and tents standing. The regiment was at once ordered to advance, but cautiously. The troops jumped the breastworks and filed through the Rebel abbatis, and the race for Richmond began. Lieut.-Col. Torrance reports that companies G and C of the 29th were, without doubt, the first companies of infantry to enter the city.

The regiment remained in Richmond a few days and was then ordered to Petersburg, thence to Point Lookout, Md., where it remained until June 10th, when it embarked with the 25th Corps for Texas, arriving at Brazos De Santiago July 3, 1865. From thence it marched to Brownsville on the Rio Grande, where it continued until ordered to Hartford, Conn., for muster-out.

The regiment was discharged and paid at Hartford, on the 25th of November, 1865, having faithfully upheld the honor of the State, and warranting the assertion that "The colored troops fought nobly!"

ITS ENGAGEMENTS WERE

Near Pittsburg, Va., Aug. 13, to Sept. 24, 1864; *Advance on Richmond, Va.*, Sept. 29 to Oct. 1, 1864; *Darbytown Road, Va.*, Oct. 13, 1864; *Kell House, Va.*, Oct. 27 and 28, 1864.

ITS CASUALTIES WERE

Killed in action, 23; died of wounds, 22; died of disease, 153; discharged prior to muster-out of regiment, 135; Total, 333.

TO THE VISITORS

AND

BROTHER SOLDIERS AND VETERANS,

GEELEY, THE CLOTHIER

Invites one and all to visit him at Nos. 115 to 119 ASYLUM Street, where he keeps constantly on hand a fine assortment of Men's, Youths', and Boys' CLOTHING at reasonable prices.

GEELEY, CLOTHIER

Nos. 115 to 119

ASYLUM STREET.

THIRTIETH REGIMENT.

Part of the Thirty-First U. S. Colored Troops.

This regiment was organized during the winter of 1863-4. It was never filled to the maximum, and only four companies were finally organized. Those were ordered to Virginia, and on the 4th of June were consolidated with the 31st U. S. colored troops, and assigned to the Ninth Army Corps. The division was in a position in rear to prevent the enemy's cavalry from attacking its rear. On the 14th it proceeded across the Chickahominy and James rivers, and marched to the front of Petersburg, remaining in that position until July 29th, without any close engagement.

On the morning of the 30th it was in line, preparatory to an assault on the enemy's works, which had been mined, and the troops, as soon as the explosion occurred, were ordered forward under a galling fire, which thinned their ranks terribly. Lieut.-Col. Ross fell, seriously wounded, while gallantly leading his regiment. Major Wright reports: "More bravery and enthusiasm I never witnessed. Besides their patriotic ardor they went into the action determined to command the respect of the white troops, which they knew could only be done by hard fighting." The regiment lost in this engagement 136 in killed and wounded.

In October it was in a severe skirmish near Fort Sedgwick, in which it lost 21 in killed and wounded.

Nov. 6th Col. H. C. Ward assumed command of the regiment. On the 18th of the same month it moved to Bermuda Hundred front, where it relieved a brigade of 100 day men, and established the picket line which they had lost. Until December it held the right of the Bermuda line, exposed to a constant and worrying fire from the enemy. During March, 1865, a detachment was sent for duty at the Dutch Gap canal, but rejoined the regiment in the movements of the spring campaign. March 27th it crossed the James, and on the 29th it was in position at Hatch's Run, upon the left of the army of the Potomac. From that time until April 3d the regiment was almost constantly under the enemy's fire, and took part in the operations on the southwest of Petersburg. On the 3d it commenced the pursuit of the enemy, which lasted six days, the regiment averaging sixteen hours' marching in every twenty-four, and in the thirty hours ending at 11 P. M., on July 8th, it achieved sixty miles. On the morning of the 9th the enemy surrendered, and from that day the regiment was not engaged.

May 25th it embarked with its corps for Texas, and disembarked at Brazos de Santiago on the 22d of June, 1865. It was engaged in garrison duty until Oct. 11th, when, being ordered for muster out, it proceeded to Hartford, and was finally discharged at that place Dec. 1, 1865.

ITS GENERAL ENGAGEMENTS.

Petersburg Mine, Va., July 30, 1864; *near Fort Sedgwick, Va.*, Oct., 1864; *Bermuda Hundred, Va.*, from Nov. 18 to Dec. 30, 1864; *before Petersburg, Va.*, from March 29 to April 2, 1865; *Surrender of Lee, Va.*, April 9, 1865.

The four companies from Connecticut suffered the following

CASUALTIES.

Killed in action,	15
Died of wounds,	4
Died of disease,	47
Discharged prior to muster out,	47
Missing at time of muster out,	13
Total,	126

THE OLD BATTLE FLAGS!

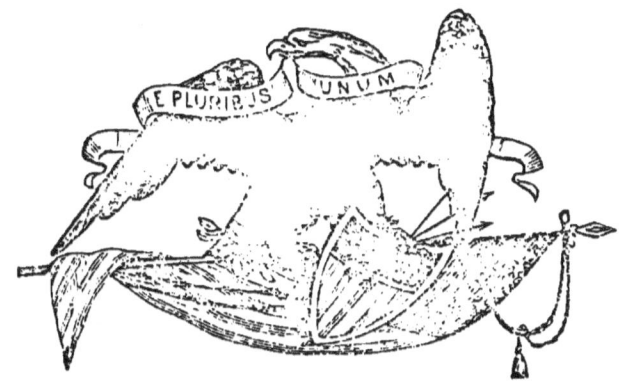

While in the Capitol City,
SEPT. 17, 1879,

To witness the Grand Pageant of the transfer of the glorious old Battle Flags to the State Capitol

Don't Forget to call on

Dealer in Foreign and Domestic

DRY GOODS,

Silks, Shawls, Dress Goods,

Cloths, White Goods, Handkerchiefs, and Gloves, Laces, Hosiery, Ladies' and Gent's Furnishing Goods, Ribbons, Prints, Small Wares, &c.,

NO. 179 MAIN STREET,

OPPOSITE ST. JOHN'S CHURCH,

HARTFORD, CONN.

GLORIOUS OLD FLAGS.

THE DAYS THEY COMMEMORATE, AND THE MEN WHO BORE THEM.

It is impossible in the limited space to give in detail the history of the battle flags; and we are indebted to the *New Haven Union* for the following: To those not familiar with the figures, it will be interesting to note what Connecticut did when these flags were at the front.

The whole number of men enlisted was 54,882, with terms of enlistment as follows:

Three months men,	2,340
Nine months men,	5,602
One year men,	529
Two years men,	25
Three years men,	44,556
Four years men,	26
Term not known,	1,804
Total,	54,882

Of this number 97 officers and 1,094 men were killed in action; 48 officers and 663 men died from wounds; 63 officers and 3,426 men died from disease; 21 officers and 889 men were "missing." Fifty-two Connecticut men rose to be general officers during the war, and the list is as follows:

Colonel and Brevet Major-General Henry L. Abbott; Major-General Henry W. Benham, Meriden; Brevet Major-General Henry W. Birge, Norwich; Brigadier-General Luther P. Bradley, New Haven; Brevet Brigadier-General Erastus Blakeslee, Plymouth; Brigadier-General Henry B. Carrington; Brigadier-General William T. Clark, Norwalk; Major-General Darius N. Couch, Danbury; Brevet Brigadier-General William G. Ely, Norwich; Brevet Brigadier-General Theodore G. Ellis, Hartford; Brigadier-General Orris S. Ferry, Norwalk; Lieut.-Colonel and Brevet Brigadier-General E. D. S. Goodyear, North Haven; Brevet Brigadier-General Edwin S. Greeley, New Haven; Brigadier-General Edward Harland, Norwich; Brevet Major-General Joseph R. Hawley, Hartford; Brevet Brigadier-General James Hubbard, Salisbury; Brigadier-General Henry M. Judah, Westport; Brigadier-General William S. Ketchum; Brigadier-General Nathaniel Lyon, Eastford; Brevet Brigadier-General Edward M. Lee, Guilford; Brevet Brigadier-General Gustavus Loomis, Stratford; Brevet Brigadier-General John Loomis, Windsor; Major-General Joseph K. F. Mansfield, Middletown; Major-General Joseph A. Mower, New London; Brigadier-General Ranold S. Mackenzie; Major-General Newton; Brevet Brigadier-General William H. Noble, Bridgeport; Brevet Brigadier-General John L. Otis, Manchester; Brevet Brigadier-General Joseph C. Perkins, New London; Brevet Brigadier-General William S. Pierson, Windsor; Brigadier-General James W. Ripley; Brigadier-General Benjamin S. Roberts, New Haven; Brevet Brigadier-General Alfred P. Rockwell, Norwich; Brevet

Brigadier-General Samuel Ross; Major-General John Sedgwick, Cornwall; Brigadier-General Truman Seymour; Brevet Brigadier-General Griffin A. Stedman, Hartford; Brigadier-General A. Von Steinwehr, Wallingford; Brevet Major-General Alexander Shaler; Major-General Alfred H. Terry, New Haven; Brigadier-General Alfred Tyler, Norwich; Brigadier-General H. D. Terry; Brevet Major-General Joseph G. Totten, New London; Brevet Brigadier-General John E. Tourtelotte, Thompson; Brevet Major-General Robert O. Tyler, Hartford; Brevet Major-General Henry W. Wessells, Litchfield; Major-General Horatio G. Wright, Clinton; Brevet Major-General A S. Williams; Brevet Brigadier-General Edward W. Whitaker, Ashford; Brevet Brigadier-General Henry M. Whittlesey; Brevet Brigadier-General Henry C. Ward.

When some of these, with the veterans of lesser rank, march on the 17th of September from the Arsenal, there will be left behind several flags which have seen battle. One was taken, according to an inscription, at the battle of Irish Bend, La., April 14, 1863, by the Thirteenth C. V. Another flag was taken at Fort Pulaski by Major-General Hunter, April 11, 1862. Another was taken at Morris Island, July 10, 1863, by the Sixth C. V., Colonel J. S. Chatfield. A card says that the Sixth charged alone on the enemy's batteries; a Southerner started to run with the flag; the Colonel twice told him to stop, but he kept on, when Private Roper Hunslow of Co. D, Sixth C. V., shot him through the head, and he fell on the flag, staining it with his life-blood. Another was taken at Pocotaligo, October 22, 1862. There is also a regimental flag; a Southern "national" flag taken from the Fourth Mississippi by Captain William Wright of the Ninth C. V., at Pass Christian, Mississippi, April 4, 1862. It was made by the ladies of Pass Christian and presented to the regiment. It is made of silk and bears a magnolia. The Connecticut flags will be placed in cases which will allow them to be unfolded in the State Capitol. The others will remain. Perhaps the sunlight will touch them tenderly for the bravery of those who once stood under them, but they are flags of "The Lost Cause."

DARCY'S

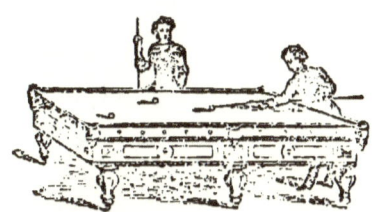

ALLYN HALL
Billiard and Pool Room

ALLYN HALL BUILDING, HARTFORD

EIGHT TABLES

OF THE MOST APPROVED MAKES,

The handsomest place in the City to enjoy a game of Billiards or Pool.

P. DARCY.

THE STAR-SPANGLED BANNER.

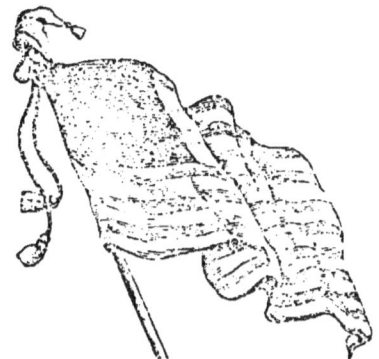

Oh! say, can you see, by the dawn's early light,
   What so proudly we hail'd at the twilight's last gleaming;
Whose broad stripes and bright stars through the perilous fight,
   O'er the ramparts we watch'd, were so gallantly streaming;
And the rocket's red glare, the bombs bursting in air,
   Gave proof through the night that our flag was still there:
Oh! say does the star-spangled banner still wave,
   O'er the land of the free, and the home of the brave?

On the shore, dimly seen through the mist of the deep,
   Where the foe's haughty host in dread silence reposes,
What is that which the breeze o'er the towering steep,
   As it fitfully blows, half conceals, half discloses?
Now it catches the gleam of the morning's first beam?
   In full glory reflected, now shines on the stream;
'Tis the star-spangled banner, O! long may it wave,
   O'er the land of the free, and the home of the brave.

And where is the band who so vauntingly swore
   That the havoc of war, and the battle's confusion,
A home and a country should leave us no more,
   Their blood has washed out their foul footstep's pollution.
No refuge could save the hireling and slave,
   From the terror of flight or the gloom of the grave;
And the star-spangled banner in triumph shall wave,
   O'er the land of the free, and the home of the brave.

Oh! thus be it ever, when freemen shall stand
   Between their loved home and war's desolation;
Bless'd with victory and peace, may the heaven-rescu'd land
   Praise the power that hath made and preserv'd us a nation!
Then conquer we must, when our cause it is just,
   And this be our motto, "In God is our trust!"
And the star-spangled banner in triumph shall wave,
   O'er the land of the free, and the home of the brave.

THROW AWAY THE OLD HAT!

And call and select a NEW ONE from the Large
and Fashionable Fall Stock of

HATS AND CAPS

TO BE FOUND AT

E. L. PARKER'S,

WHOLESALE AND RETAIL DEALER IN

Hats, Caps, Furs, Robes, Gloves, &c.

109 ASYLUM STREET,
HARTFORD, CONN.

THE CASE, LOCKWOOD & BRAINARD CO.

PRINTERS, BINDERS,

AND MANUFACTURERS OF

DIARIES FOR 1880.

SPECIAL ATTENTION GIVEN TO

✻ ILLUSTRATED ✛ CATALOGUE ✛ WORK ✻

HARTFORD, CONN.

COR. PEARL AND TRUMBULL STS.